THE BOSSY GIRL'S GUIDE TO LEADERSHIP

THE BOSSY GIRL'S GUIDE TO LEADERSHIP

Real Talk on Power, Purpose, and Leading Out Loud

Michelle Marquis

Published by Game Changer Publishing

Paperback ISBN: 978-1-968250-50-8

Hardcover ISBN: 978-1-968250-51-5

Digital ISBN: 978-1-968250-52-2

www.GameChangerPublishing.com

To my daughters, Sienna and Mikala—your voices are fierce, your hearts are full, and your leadership inspires me daily. Watching you lead in your own bold ways is one of my greatest joys and proudest legacies.

To my husband of thirty-seven years, for encouraging me through my growth and being the biggest cheerleader on my squad.

To all the Bossy Girls who didn't have a strong example of what women could do but kept showing up and earning it until they learned it, this is for you.

To the Bossy Girls I've leaned on, learned from, laughed with, and cried with—thank you for reminding me that I was never alone.

And to my mom, your strength shaped mine. Through every hard choice and sacrifice, you gave me the tools to rise. I am the woman and leader I am today because of you. I see you. I thank you. I love you.

May this book be a mirror and a megaphone for every woman who's ever questioned her self-worth and a reminder that your power has always been yours to claim. No matter what others think.

READ THIS FIRST

Just to say thanks for buying and reading my book, I would love to connect with you and provide you with the accompanying workbook!

Scan the QR Code Here:

SCAN ME

THE BOSSY GIRL'S Guide to LEADERSHIP

REAL TALK ON POWER, PURPOSE, AND LEADING OUT LOUD

MICHELLE MARQUIS

FOREWORD

When I think about Michelle Marquis, the first words that come to mind are "strength" and "presence"—naturally earned presence. Her leadership story is raw, reflecting what so many women in business experience behind the scenes but rarely talk about out loud.

The ladders we get to climb today were built by Michelle and women like her, who carried the weight of outdated expectations, quiet biases, and stories they will probably never tell.

But the beauty of Michelle's story is that she is a woman who chooses to grow again and again with integrity, grit and a deep courage that she earned, no matter what life throws at her or what puddle she might misstep into.

I've had the privilege of watching Michelle evolve over the years. She has always had a sharp business mind, but she also never settles and is always seeking new opportunities and growth. She leans into discomfort and is unbothered by what some may deem overwhelming, always leading through action.

I remember encouraging Michelle to simply be vulnerable and tell her story to her readers. And boy, did she step up to the plate! Michelle peels back the layers we often hide: the impostor syndrome, the second-guessing, the moments when being "bossy" feels like the only way to survive. She tells the truth about what it's like to be a woman who wants to do good work, lead well, and not lose herself in the process.

You'll walk away from *The Bossy Girl's Guide to Leadership* with a deeper understanding of what it takes to lead authentically *and* sustainably. You'll see your own stories in Michelle's and start to rewrite the inner narratives that have kept you playing small. So, I invite you to see this book as a mirror that reflects your own innate power, if you're willing to own it.

Michelle took the hits that many of us are still ducking. She said the things that others were too afraid to say. And in doing so, she cleared a path for women in business to have a little more room, a little more agency, and a little more truth. So I invite you to dive into her real talk on "power, purpose, and leading out loud."

If you've ever questioned whether you belong in the room, this book will remind you that you've always had a seat at the table. You just need to pull all the way up.

– Amber Hurdle
CEO, Amber Hurdle Consulting
Author, *The Bombshell Business Woman: How to Become a Bold, Brave Female Entrepreneur*

CONTENTS

PREFACE

One of the most impactful times when I felt like I was not enough (to love, to matter, to be important) occurred when I was about thirteen. My mom had sent my sister and me to live with my grandmother in Pacific Palisades while she studied for the bar exam. My father lived not far away from where I was living, but very rarely (if ever) visited.

On my thirteenth birthday, he told me he was going to come visit me and bring me a birthday present, and he asked me what the one thing I wanted was. I shared that I wanted a record holder to keep my 45s in. These records, seven-inch vinyl singles that played at 45 RPM, had one song on each side, and collecting them was kind of a "thing" in 1976. My favorite at the time was by a band named Kiss with a song called "Beth" on one side and "Detroit Rock City" on the other. I share that because it's so funny that I still remember this! He promised me he would bring me that record holder.

I woke up early, did my hair, and got ready for his visit. Yes, I wanted the birthday present, but I also wanted to see him so he could be proud of his little girl, all grown up. He had told me he would arrive at 10:30

a.m., so I was outside on the front steps by 10:00. As I waited, I went in and out of the house dozens of times during the day to see what time it was. We spoke a few times throughout the day, and he kept telling me he was running late but on his way. By the third time I called, he stopped answering.

I waited all day for him to come, but he never did. I remember going into my room and crying until I fell asleep. I did not understand why he did not love me. The feeling of not being enough and having to prove myself over and over again began before my thirteenth birthday, but this memory still brings me to tears.

This book is for everyday women striving to be good leaders who possess the doubts of "impostor syndrome," "I-am-not-special syndrome," or "I am not _____ enough" (fill in the blank with their own negative self-talk). I have and sometimes still do suffer from the same negative thinking—I just pushed through the many emotional and mental pivots to keep my head above water and create stepping stones from stumbling blocks.

What gave me the courage to embark on this book? A couple of years ago, I was asked to deliver a keynote address at a women's conference by Amy Hinote, a successful woman leader in her own right and someone I greatly respected. I was so proud, but the minute after I said yes, I had second thoughts. Similar doubts crossed my mind while writing this book. As Amy and I discussed the possibility and topics, she said, "If you do this, you need to pull back the mask. People think they know you. Show them who you really are."

That is when I thought, *Who do people think I am, as opposed to who I really am? How do I show the face behind the mask without knowing this distinction?*

As I prepared, I began journaling, answering the questions: "Who am I? What do others think I am? What is behind the mask?" A flood of negative thoughts came to my mind. Those included not only what I believed other people thought I was, but also how that compared to what I thought about myself. I realize that I believed so many negative things about myself.

To speak at a Women's Conference had been something that I had always wanted to do—a BHAG (big, hairy, audacious goal). That speech was the start of this book.

Many inspiring talks and books come from women who have done *big* things in their lives. I will not cure cancer or build a Fortune 500 company. I am an ordinary mom, wife, sister, daughter, breadwinner, leader, friend, and mentor. I have faced some challenges in life, many of which some of you might relate to. The stories I have here are not only to show how I overcame them, but also how they were foundational to my success. I've had success in my life, in part, *because* of the life hurdles I've encountered. It might have been easier to sit back and let life happen to me; instead, I wanted to prove to myself, my mom, my dad, and society that I could be successful even with all the circumstances I've faced.

It felt like everything leading up to this point had been fighting to keep me doubting myself, yet somewhere deep inside of me, I didn't believe that lie anymore. In fact, I had already begun to start building the life I truly wanted—as a woman, wife, future mother, and female business leader. While the pains of my childhood would forever paint the backdrop of my story, I had come to realize with clarity that **I was now the painter**, not my dad, my mom, or even the thoughts inside my mind.

From broken and rejected to empowered and influential, this is my story, and I know that I'm not alone. Countless female leaders have been built from the ashes of childhood trauma, but make no mistake, that path to success must be chosen.

CHAPTER 1
POSTER CHILD FOR NOT ENOUGH

don't have many vivid memories of when my parents were married, and the ones I do have are not pleasant. The sounds streamed into the bedroom I shared with my little sister, muffled, but clearly angry. I lay quietly in my twin bed, listening to what my parents were saying. I was frightened by the yelling and screaming. My dad would escalate quickly when he was angry about something, and that taught me to be "small" and invisible. However, I was not scared enough to stay in bed and ignore the fighting that was going on.

At only six, I was keenly aware of the implications that fighting had in our household, but I still crept out of bed and crawled through the hallway to an opening in the slats of the wall heater. In the late '60s, we did not yet have centralized heating; the heater was built between walls so it could push air through to multiple rooms of the house. There was dust between the slats, and the air smelled old and was warm on my face. These slats allowed me not only to hear more clearly, but they also allowed a sneak peek from one room to the other if you squinted at just the right angle.

I sat there, watching my mom and my dad argue over a red, black, and white booklet. I didn't understand the importance of the book, but I knew my dad wanted it badly. My dad would do whatever he had to get his hands on that book, and at this moment, the only thing in his way was my mom. The next thing I remember was my dad literally throwing my mom across the room and into a wall. The yelling was something I was used to; the physical abuse was not. I believe this memory is a part of who I am today, and it's why I don't want anyone to be mad at me, and I try to fix problems before they escalate.

While pieces of this story are lost forever in my memory, I vividly remember one particular Christmas morning. Knowing that they were fighting about that little red-and-black-checkered booklet, I wrapped it up for him for Christmas. As I reflect on this memory, it also makes me wonder if it had an impact on one of my love languages: gifts. One of our traditions to this day is opening one gift at a time. I waited patiently for it to be his turn, and I watched excitedly as he unwrapped his gift from me. I think he was confused, but he must have pretended he liked it. What I didn't know at the time was that the little book was a checkbook. I just thought he wanted the booklet—what he desperately wanted was the money in the checking account. My mom knew we needed the money for food, and he wanted it for booze and partying.

The fighting and abuse (physically and mentally) continued to be a part of my parents' relationship. The town they lived in at the time was small. My dad had been an athlete and a "man around town." Everywhere we went, there was someone who knew him.

So, not long after that Christmas, my mom packed up our red Chevy Impala with all the essentials we would need to abandon what we knew and embrace the uncertain future. My mom had to leave behind her entire family and friends to start a new life. She drove north until people wouldn't know who she was. Our family of three survived by raising each other, relying on food stamps, low-income housing, and the FIO (figure it out) factor.

FIO is discussed in great detail later, but we learned about it very early on.

I am beyond proud of the woman my mother is and the hardships that she not only faced but overcame to raise the two of us. Like most women of her generation, my mother was raised to become a wife and a mother. She attended college with the sole purpose of finding a husband. When she became pregnant out of wedlock, she had little choice but to marry her high school sweetheart, my dad.

This meant that living in Northern California was the first time my mother was faced with the struggles of not only raising herself and learning to live on her own, but raising a five-year-old and a seven-year-old without any means of support.

During the day, she worked as a secretary at a law firm, and at night, she switched hats to bartend, all while attending law school. Years later, when I asked her how she managed it all, she told me, "Michelle, I just did what I had to do. I figured it out." Unbeknownst to me at the time, this would quickly become a recurring theme for my future. She figured out how to raise me as she did it! She was my example of just trudging forward.

While I'm extremely proud of my mother, the fact that my sister and I faced numerous struggles as a result of the choices she had to make is not lost on me. The FIO factor showed up everywhere for me. I was quick to understand that for anything I wanted, I just had to make things happen.

About ten years ago, I got a Facebook message from someone named Bonnie, asking if my last name was previously Saenz and if I had a sister. When I told her yes, she said, "I wanted to thank you for something you did for me when I was about ten." She went on to say, "We had no money for a tree or Christmas gifts. You went door to door, asking for work, can collections, or donations to help our family."

How did I know what to do or say to make this happen? I just figured it out. I once had a colleague say to me, "Michelle, you are always trying to get around the bush to make things happen."

I replied, "I do not think you meant that as a compliment, but I will take it as one."

When I want something to happen, I get creative about how to do it. I guess I have always felt there is a "way" to figure out life's problems. My experiences have shown me this.

My sister and I were left to fend for ourselves. They would have called us latch-key kids, but we were more than that. We were alone a lot. This ended up with me being "in charge" of my sister, with a large responsibility very early on, and there was an intense parentification switch amongst the family. I was responsible for ensuring we had dinner (including preparing it), completed our homework, took baths, and went to bed on time on the nights my mom went to school or worked at the bar. During the summer, it also meant being in charge of my sister, sometimes for more than twenty-four hours at a time.

I had major responsibilities at too young an age—I still remember what could/couldn't be purchased with food stamps. At the time, I took this role as just part of my responsibilities, but as I grew older, I was put in an impossible position. I had too much power too soon. I didn't understand my role as I transitioned from being a kid to being the "responsible" one. For as long as I can remember, I was always the responsible one, the one to follow the rules. I will put my toe on that line, but I will figure out a way to get things done within the rules. It's just what I've always done. Is it because I had some sort of control when I was in charge? Did it allow me to control the outcome? I had nobody to rely on, so this followed me through life. Without guidance, did this behavior come across as bossy and abrasive?

I could write an entire book on the complications that being "the little parent" had on my relationship with my sister, and my future relationships as a whole, but I will acknowledge this: I was cruel to my sister. As any good therapist would tell you, these traumas from my childhood would go on to impact all areas of my life, good and bad. I am not sure her and my relationship will ever be repaired. There is just too much pain, for both of us.

As I share some of my life stories with you, you'll see that I experienced more than my fair share of traumas. Many of them, I had to overcome by simply pushing forward and using the FIO factor. I want to share these events in my life because they taught me valuable lessons. I am aware that everyone fights their own battles, and these are mine.

As terrible a husband as my father was, my mom never said a bad word about him. She wanted us to build our own relationships with him, unencumbered by her experiences. I wish she hadn't. Through my dad, I learned lessons about abandonment, loss, disappointment, and that I was not enough. He was an addict, and he chose alcohol and drugs over being a father to my sister and me. I recognize now that my father had a disease and his own traumas, but as a young girl, all I understood was the absence of a father figure.

After my parents divorced, we saw him very little. He constantly made promises that he wouldn't keep. He promised and failed to visit, send a birthday card, call, send Christmas presents, attend graduation, and even walk me down the aisle. His absence fed the voice in my head that told me I was not enough.

When I was around forty-five, my father was on his way to visit us in Oregon, and I was so excited. He lived in Hawaii and was already on the mainland, so there was very little chance he wouldn't show. I was so proud of the life my husband and I had created, and I wanted my dad to be proud of me, too. At that point, I had an eight-year-old and a thirteen-year-old, was working as a sales director, and had a nice home, a wonderful husband, and an overall successful life. I wanted my father to see his little girl as the successful woman she had become.

The evening before he was supposed to arrive, he called and canceled. I had been preparing for this with years of therapy, and I thought I was okay with it. It was nothing new; I'd been prepared to expect disappointment when it came to him my entire life. Later that night, my husband woke me up because I was crying in my sleep. In my sleep, I was just a thirteen-year-old little girl waiting for him, only to be disappointed. With tears running down my face, I realized that I was not ready for this. I thought, *Why am I not good enough for him to love, no matter what I accomplish?* I was not **enough**.

Growing up without my father's involvement led to a deep feeling of abandonment. I wished every day for the hole to be filled—even dreamed of my mom and dad getting back together. It wasn't just my father I wanted, but someone to fill the role of a father figure.

As a result, when my mom dated and brought men home to meet us, my sister and I were quick to think that this could be the start of a new life and the family unit that we so desperately wanted. The reality of the situation, however, was that the men were just boyfriends who came and went. My sister and I, I am sure, scared many away. We just wanted a father. I am not even sure we knew or understood what that meant, but there was a gap in what it meant to have a father involved in our lives.

" If you look deep into the soul of a strong independent woman, you may find a broken little girl who had to learn to get back up and never depend on anyone. "

When I saw this saying, I quickly resonated with it: "There are very few women I meet who are strong, independent, and scary (to others) who were not a broken little girl who had to learn to get back up and not depend on anyone."

Years later, I was at my mom's sixtieth birthday party, and several men she had dated were in attendance. I remember being so excited about seeing some of these men who had meant so much to me in my younger years. As I got to talking with them, I realized that most of them barely remembered me. They'd had such big places in my life, but to them, I was just a brief moment in their lives. It was kind of eye-opening.

That said, not all the men she brought home were safe. In my fifties, I had a memory about something that had been repressed since I was very young. One of the men she brought home taught me how to play guitar. He also molested me. I know this story can be hard for many to face, and it was for me, too. However, I share this with you because it is a part of my story and has impacted the way I trust people, my feelings about men, and how I continue to live my life.

Mom did meet somebody whom she fell in love with. He was tall and handsome, and he made her happy. They were together for six weeks before they got married. Oh, and I forgot to mention, he was twenty-three. At the time, I was seventeen, and my sister was fifteen.

I was so excited at first, thinking that I finally had the father figure I had dreamed of. However, there were signs early on that not only was he not going to change our family dynamics, but he was also going to cause us significant harm. The stress of raising two teenagers who had not had a father figure in the house became apparent, and his behavior started to change.

He gaslighted my mom into believing things about us that were just not true. The lies were small at first, like telling us to be home by 10:00 p.m., finding out that the curfew was 9:00 p.m. while we were out, and then yelling at us that we were supposed to be home by 9:00 p.m. That way, he was not in trouble with Mom, but I would be grounded because I came home at 10:00 p.m., as he'd told me I could. He would permit me to do different things, like drive to the beach, but when I got home, he would blatantly lie and say that he'd specifically told me I was not allowed to go. This became a theme that would drive a wedge between my mother and me. She believed everything he told her and distrusted my sister and me.

I saw his manipulation, the way he spent the whole day high, while my mom was at work, and he would hide the worst parts of himself from her. Though it was so obvious to me, my mom could not see beyond the handsome young man he was.

The day that they got married, I shared how I felt with my mom, and my aunt slapped me hard across the face—my mom just let it happen. I felt like I was gaining the "father figure" I had always craved and possibly losing my mom, her love, and trust. I was scared and felt so alone. Alone also meant not safe. Safety, security, or the lack of it, was something that had followed me my whole life. This was a real "aha" moment for me.

Within about two months of their marriage, we ended up going to family counseling. During the counseling sessions, he would continue to lie about the things he said and did to both me and my sister, and my mom believed him and supported him. I confessed in therapy that he had been making us do intense physical labor (he made us pull out crabgrass, clump by clump, with our bare hands until our fingers were raw) all while he sat inside, smoking. My mom still didn't believe me.

It all came to a head between my mom and me because she continued to believe him over me. The wedge between us seemed insurmountable. In one counseling session, she told me that she had finished raising me. I was now grown up, and she had done all that she could for me. She said that it was time that she finally focused on herself instead of on me.

I was told that I could live by all of their rules and continue living at home, or I could move out. Because of "Bongo Dad" (we called him that because he sat in front of his bong most of the day while my mom went to work and we went to school), the rules were always changing, and I simply had no choice but to move out. I was seventeen. My father and mother had both chosen someone or something over me, and I was alone. Not safe. Not secure.

At just seventeen and still in high school, I had to support myself. This meant that I went from being part of a family to being alone and unsupported financially, mentally, physically, and practically. I went from kid to grown-up in the span of a few weeks. I was lucky enough to have a family that allowed me to stay with them. Try to imagine this. I had to pack up my room, load my car, and stay with another family (who had little money to support another mouth) until I could find an apartment and a job that also allowed me to continue with school and play sports. All I remember was that I had no choice other than to march forward. I told myself,

Don't slow down, and don't think about it too much.
When you feel you are not enough, you feel unloved.
When you feel unloved, you feel you are not safe.
When you feel unsafe, you become scared.
When you are scared, you tend to be in a constant state of
fight or flight.
When you want to fight or flee, you are in a state of "being
on edge."
When you are on edge, you try to be alert and ahead of
whatever is coming at you.
This led to my staying ahead of things and just FIO.

This experience was just another example of me feeling I was not enough to be loved, considered, and supported. The experience of wanting to fight or flee has recurred in various areas of my life, including jobs, friendships, and even my thirty-seven-year marriage to my husband, Brian. At that time in my life, I was faced with the realities of what it meant to use the FIO factor. I just had to go FIO because mom didn't support me living at home, but she also didn't support me moving out.

I recall a time when it became challenging for me to balance everything (working, going to school, playing sports, and just being grown up too soon), and I called my mom and asked to come home. When she told me no, I was devastated. She picked my stepfather over me again. The saddest part of the whole thing is that their marriage was over in about three years.

Why did I crave that validation from a father figure? I have learned (through counseling, books, and relationships I trust) that girls who grow up without a strong male influence can end up with low self-esteem and look for validation in other people, specifically men, to feel worthy. Going deep here, but for many years, I used my sexuality (blond hair, blue eyes, pretty, big boobs, long legs and use of flattery bordering on flirting) as a "hook" with my male counterparts. Then I would show them that I was smart to sell them my ideas or products.

If you stopped reading here, you might think, *WTF? That is crazy. How could your mom do this?* Over the years, my mom and I have had many conversations about my childhood. She has shared that we kids were the most important thing in her life. She had every intention of keeping us safe, secure, and feeling loved. I do believe she believes this, but I also know hindsight is 20/20, and she wishes she had made some different decisions. Now, having said that, I would not be the person I am without the life I have lived.

They say that forgiveness releases *you* from the pain. I wish I had an encouraging, happy ending here. This is a work in progress for me. I have come to realize that each experience in my life has given me an edge toward success. In part, I have been able to adapt to hurdles in my life *because* of my experiences.

CHAPTER 2
PUZZLE PIECES

Before my second daughter was born, I was asked to serve on the Commission for Children and Families. This was a nonprofit organization whose board was composed of people nominated by the community, who were then interviewed and appointed by a district judge. The organization did amazing things, and I was able to really make a difference in my community. The organization focused on investing "upstream." Where could the investments be made in our community *before* there were more complicated and expensive problems to solve? A part of that discussion was around resiliency factors. Why did siblings with the same background have very different paths? What made one child more resilient than another?

I had every opportunity to head down a road of alcohol and drug abuse. I even had reasons why that could have made sense, given the traumas I have experienced. This leads me to wonder how much of who I am comes from the lessons I learned and how much is from who I am innately. It is the age-old question of *nature* versus *nurture*, whether a person's characteristics are primarily influenced by their genetic inheritance ("nature") or their environment and life experiences ("nurture") throughout development.

I think that nature is only a small part of how leaders find their way. I knew nothing of my genetics. I have been 100 percent affected by my "experiences." Nurture may come in both good and bad lessons. Many of my strengths stem from my life experiences, which is such a hard thing to think about for me. I may be *stronger, smarter,* and even *more than enough* because:

I had no father figure.
I had no support as a young adult.
I had to go about life, solving one challenge after another.
I felt abandoned.
I felt unworthy.
I felt like I was not enough.
I felt insecure.
I was scared.

All of my traumas are woven into my personality. It is hard to imagine that the stories in this book actually helped make me a better person and leader. I had to apply all the life lessons I learned to overcome the challenges I faced and not let them hold me back.

When recalling some of the decisions I've made in life to do the hard work, I've often thought, *Why didn't I just quit? It would have been so much easier.* I think it was because I had to unknowingly take control to make myself feel worthy, loved, and secure.

I am the proud mother of two strong, independent leaders who are not afraid to stand up for what they believe in, no matter the situation. Their voices have always been loud and confident. I do not think they learned this to overcome situations, but because they saw it in their mom, who, in their eyes, was just a "kick-ass" boss lady, something they and their friends referred to me as. They used to joke that their friends were afraid of me. *Good,* I thought. *Toe the line, girls.* :) Of my two daughters, the youngest one had a label put on her at a very young age: "stubborn." What I once thought was stubbornness has evolved into a strength of confidence and determination that I now admire and appreciate.

Although most of my life experiences have affected who I am today, one particularly impactful event occurred very late in life. My father is part Mexican, and we had a rich lineage and history, as well as extensive documentation of our family's history in California, including our migration through Phoenix from Mexico.

I was proud to have Hispanic heritage for many reasons. My father always told me stories about how my blue eyes came from our family's origins in northern Spain. I knew that I was an eighth-generation Californian. There is a major road in Southern California named Rose Avenue. That street was named after my great-great-great-grandmother Rose Peralta. The name Peralta is all over California history, something I was very proud of.

I have always been interested in genealogy and decided to explore the other nationalities in my bloodline. So, about ten years ago, I took the 23andMe test. When the results came back indicating that I was 99.9 percent Northern European, I initially thought nothing of it, except for disappointment that they were incorrect. I called my mom to joke about it, and we all laughed, saying, "Lucy, you have some explaining to do." This was a reference to the *I Love Lucy* show, where her husband would say that phrase when Lucy was in trouble, which was often.

I did not give this any more thought until years later, when my sister took the 23andMe test. She called me in a panic, asking me to log in and "fix" the results because it told her I was either her aunt or half-sibling. "Fix it? I haven't even looked at this in years." I had not logged into 23andMe since my initial findings and had to call the company to access my page. Lo and behold, it said that we shared 28 percent of our DNA.

I thought there had to be a mistake. My youngest daughter did a little bit of research and called my husband and said, "I'm worried about Mom. There is no way that Aunt [my sister] and Mom are full sisters. Just not possible." My husband told me about her fears, and as a result, I went on Google, and it stated that it's not possible to be full sisters, and that 28 percent of shared DNA is, in fact, indicative of half-siblings. This called into question not only my relationship with my sister but my entire identity.

Amid my panic attack, I called my mom and said, "Mom, is there any possible way that Dad could not be my father?"

She broke down crying. "I'm so sorry," she said. "I never thought anybody would find out. I never wanted you to know. I told your father there was a possibility, and we fought about it a couple of times, but we never spoke of it again. I just never thought in a million years that there'd be a way to find out this information."

This triggered a flood of emotions about who I truly was. *Is that why my dad was so abusive to himself and others? Was he mad? Does he really know? Does he not know?* A memory that quickly came to me, and that I have thought of hundreds of times since, was that my father used to share with me the story of how I had blue eyes. It was like he was trying to convince himself throughout my life that he was my father. You see, he has brown eyes, and my mother has green. While genetically possible, it was highly improbable, if not rare.

I think he has been convincing himself the whole time that he was my father. Our relationship has been and is complicated, and this has added another layer to that complexity. He doesn't know that it has been confirmed that he is not my father, and he doesn't know that I am even aware of it. He boasts of my accomplishments because it is good for his ego and some of his beliefs; therefore, the results in my life are a result of how he showed up as a father, which was not really the case at all. What keeps ringing in my ears is that I just wanted a father all along.

Shortly after thinking this through, I thought, *Wait. Who is my father? Could I have had that father figure all along? Did I miss out on an opportunity to know my biological father? What would my story have been had I known who my real father was, and had he known that I existed? Would he have been there for me? Would my entire life have been different? Would it have been easier?* I felt resentment at not having the opportunity to find the answer to these questions. I felt I had been cheated, and I was mad at my mom for not letting me know the truth sooner. This was another example of my mom choosing her safety and comfort over mine, another betrayal.

Then I realized, as much as my father had not chosen to be part of my life, he had chosen me, in a way. He knew there was a possibility that he was not the father, yet he still chose to try to be one. I have chosen not to share any of this with him (he is alive, and I hope this will remain a secret between me and my readers), but I struggle because I want him to know that I see that he stood up for me when it counted most. The questions about what could have been are endless in my mind. I have also had to come to terms with the fact that, of the two people in my family, I don't even have the connection to my sister that I thought I did. I felt like I lost so much in learning this; I lost my identity, and I lost pieces of my family.

Mikala, my youngest daughter, was a sleuth like no other. She did all of the research to find first relatives via Facebook, and then my uncle's name, which led to my father's name. Well, what the heck, I picked up the phone and dialed. As I waited for him to answer, I was nervous and hoped he would embrace the situation with open arms. Which he did, at first. He and his wife said things like, "Wow, a bonus daughter. What are you doing for Christmas?" I was so excited that I might have found the missing piece I had been looking for. I sent pictures of myself as a child. I offered to take a paternity test from a doctor, but based on the pictures, he said, "Nope, you are a [last name]."

When I finally had the opportunity to meet my biological father (BF), he was in his eighties. I drove to Sun Valley, Idaho, to meet him and two of my siblings. We first met at a kind of sterile restaurant. I arrived first and sat facing the door. When my father walked in, I was shocked because I saw my blue eyes, my high cheekbones, and chin on his face. I never thought that I didn't look like my BCF (birth certificate father), until I saw my BF (bio father).

We talk probably once a month or so. The conversations are usually the same because he's getting to a point where he doesn't remember everything. I also learned that I had another half-sibling. That meant I had a total of four siblings. Much of what I learned about my BF has been from one of my sisters. It sounds like he was very similar to my BCF in many ways and probably could not have been the "father figure" I wanted, either, but I will never know, will I? This is just another experience that has pushed me to evaluate all of my traumas and how many experiences have shaped how I act, lead, and love. I was not enough to be loved by him or my new siblings. Obviously, in reality, I know this is nothing personal, but it sure feels crummy.

While considering the realities of nature versus nurture, I realized that these play a significant role in shaping who I am versus who I could have been. For one, my nature is not what I thought it was. I was not born to a Hispanic father with drug abuse issues. None of his genetics were mine; that said, I also have to come to terms with the fact that my nurture had the chance to be very different. The nurture that I did have was foundational to who I am. In the end, I am who I am because of each of these pieces of the whole puzzle.

Nurture comes from everything that is put into your life as you mature. Society certainly has its opinion on who women should be. In the '70s and '80s, most women were wives who raised the kids and kept the home. The men got to decide how women's roles were defined. I am lucky to have had a strong and powerful mom who pushed herself to get further education and to show me, through her actions, just how much could be done. I knew that women could do anything. I never thought there were boundaries to what I could accomplish. The only things holding me back were the stories I told myself. I was never afraid of the societal boundaries or what I could accomplish.

Even today, girls are raised to be quiet, have manners, be polite (even if that means doing things they do not want to do), and not speak up. Since we have to juggle our negative thoughts and those preconceived notions of what women should be, it is no wonder that there are so many of us "doubting Michelles." We have the cards stacked against us from the start due to societal expectations.

To become a powerful woman leader, it's essential to apply those life lessons and not accept doubts, but instead, overcome them. You also need the courage and bravery to overcome these things. In my opinion, the importance of having women in leadership is that we can empower one another in whichever way we choose.

I hope my life lessons will help you find a shortcut to a lighter heart and a more successful career or life, however you define it. Let's find a way to dispel some of the myths about women leaders.

CHAPTER 3
DISPELLLING THE MYTHS OF OUR INNER TALK

I am bossy.
I am abrasive.
I am emotional.
I am difficult.
I am aggressive.
I am intimidating.
I am a bitch.

'm the poster child for every toxic adjective you've ever heard about strong women. I say that because these are adjectives that have been used to describe me, I have assumed that people said them about me, or I have thought them about myself.

Women are taught throughout life to be agreeable. When little girls grow up, they are told not to be loud, not to argue, and not to talk back, especially with adults.

"Don't be bossy."

"You are so stubborn."

"She is so strong-willed."

I have a faint memory of my dad raising his hand high at me (he stopped before hitting me) because I was being "too loud." Society has hammered (literally and figuratively) these thoughts into our minds.

These descriptions tend to be associated with powerful women to diminish their value. I hate to admit that I have believed many of these (if not all) about myself for a very long time. Sometimes, I still do. Many women leaders feel that they need to temper their language so they are not labeled with some of these adjectives.

Throughout my life, I have found that the core toxic beliefs I have held about myself have become indistinguishable and interwoven with my thoughts and behaviors. These beliefs influenced my everyday choices without me even realizing it. They say hindsight is 20/20.

Sometimes, I think that because the examples in my life were women making shit happen (my mom, my grandmother, and many other women) I did not realize these labels were something that I identified with. As I advanced in my career, I became aware of how others perceive women leaders, and possibly me.

One time, I was in a meeting with the CTO, the CEO, and the head of product in one of my roles. We were having a good, long conversation and debate about some product roadmaps and the features the software needed to have. The CTO was very contrarian; he vehemently disagreed with me on everything I said, even to the point where he pounded his fist on the table. I refused to take his shit and confidently told him my thoughts and opinions on the best way forward for the company.

After the meeting, I went to my office and cried. Once I had collected myself, I went back to the CEO and said, "How could you let him speak to me that way?"

I had asked him whether this was the culture we wanted at the company, and whether he thought it was acceptable for leadership to speak to anyone with that level of disrespect. I had truly believed in the

CEO, and I was just shocked that he didn't say, "Knock it off," to the CTO.

He looked at me and said, "Michelle, you completely held your own. You didn't seem like you needed saving. You did exactly what you should have done and handled him exactly how you should have handled him, and I'm sorry."

I thought back to the words exchanged at the meeting and realized that my CEO was right; I had held my own. The next day, the CTO and I were in our board meeting waiting for a meeting to start, and he said to me, "Can I close the door?" I was apprehensive about what he was about to say, but I said yes anyway. He got up and closed the door, and then he said, "You know, when a man speaks with authority and with conviction, he's looked at as a strong leader, and when a woman does the same thing, she's looked at as a bitch. I'm sorry for the way I behaved yesterday." After reflecting on the meeting, he realized that he'd thought that I was being a bitch, which had led him to communicate with me in the way he had. In reality, I was being authoritative and speaking with conviction, the same way a man would.

I said to him, "I didn't think that you were a strong leader. I just thought you were an asshole." Don't worry—we laughed it off, and we are still good friends and mentors to one another.

I took training at one point, and it taught me that eighty percent of our thoughts on any given day are negative. Of those eighty percent of thoughts, ninety-five percent of them are on repeat. Now, I am not sure whether these numbers are accurate, or even how one would go about collecting that data; however, what I do know is that I tend to have repetitive negative thoughts about myself. If eighty percent of your thoughts are negative and ninety-five percent are on repeat, this is like having a podcast in your ears that constantly tells you bad things about yourself. Changing this is a constant battle, and it's so much easier said than done.

We get to decide how we define ourselves, how we talk to ourselves, and what voices are saying in our head. Sounds simple, right? The negative background noise for me was that I was not good enough for so many things (love, good things in my life, promotions, you name it), and that good things came to me because I was lucky. It was not until I sat down to write the speech that inspired this book that I began to challenge the notions I had about myself.

I not only used to believe these labels about myself, but I also placed a heavy weight on what others thought about me. My thoughts today are more influenced by *what I think* about myself, which has given me new freedom.

In fleshing out this book, I found myself in a discussion with one of my daughters about the core issue I am trying to convey in this chapter. Is it dispelling the myths of the words that describe me (and many other women leaders)? Some of these labels have been learned or maybe even earned throughout our lives. The only thing I can focus on, however, is how I think about myself, not what others think.

I lost a job that I knew I excelled at and one that had brought me great success. While I worked for this company, we consistently broke company-wide records, introduced new products, grew total revenue, and helped prepare the company for a very successful sale to an outside investor. If I'm being honest, there was tension, so I wasn't completely surprised. I had been to HR with some concerns. There had been rumors that I was going to be fired. The way the other leaders behaved around me had changed.

The tension was because there were two "clubs": one of people on the inside and one of people on the outside. The outside was for anyone who had a differing opinion. Because I hold people accountable (abrasive) and am direct (aggressive), transparent (intimidating), consistent (difficult), and a woman, the other club did not know how to handle me. I think they expected me to just go with the flow (and be bullied) by those with more influence. I am a truth-teller; I hold people accountable and do not back down because of pressure.

When I was fired, I doubted all of my accomplishments and, of course, doubted myself. I thought, *Why couldn't you just go with the flow while you decided what you wanted to do?* Why couldn't I just do that? It is easier, right? No, I couldn't just go with the flow because I felt strongly in my convictions of how I serve and, frankly, doing what I believe is right for my clients and team members.

But because I did not go with the flow, I felt like I had failed, not only myself but my family. Being raised on a single mother's income, living in low-income housing, surviving on food stamps, and moving out so young, I have always had financial insecurity at the forefront of my mind. For the last fifteen years, I have been the breadwinner (happily) of my family. The fear of financial instability for my daughters and my husband has been something that has often kept me awake at night. To be fired was not only very new to me, but a very real fear that I had, even as a high performer all of my life.

My immediate response after being let go was shame. I thought, *Who would want to work with me? If I am not the chief revenue officer and leader in my industry, who am I? What will people say? What will people think?* In my mind, the notoriety of the role I had was *why* people believed in me. It totally freaked me out!

The night I was fired, I couldn't sleep. I got up in the middle of the night and had my pity party of one. Then I got to work on crafting my own messaging to convey to my peers what I wanted them to understand about my next steps. I carefully and thoughtfully wrote a post on LinkedIn. I wanted the post to read positively, but also to be bold about my accomplishments. It read:

Michelle Marquis (She/Her) · You ···
I am a ShortCut2$. Simple. Consulting with Suppliers and Prope...
Request services
1yr · 🌐

Dear Peers, Clients, Partners and Friends,

For the first time in my life I find myself in a surprising and unique position.

I am "open to work" or maybe consult. Now is not the time to be shy about my achievements.

I have a reputation of being a category maker, a rain maker and can make a huge impact.
I am someone who can help propel companies and people to high levels of success. I know the short term rental industry, the players and the technology landscape like few others.

Please share this message within your networks or reach out to me.

Now is the time to show the value of my network. Ready. Set. Go.

💛👍❤️ 177   39 comments · 16 reposts

❤️ Love   💬 Comment   🔁 Repost   ✈️ Send

📊 17,931 impressions   View analytics

Based on the impressions alone, I saw that my post had made an impact. While the numbers may not seem high to some, they are equivalent to a viral post on LinkedIn. I went from feeling scared and doubting myself to feeling confident and valued. I felt true love for who I was and what I had accomplished, based on me as a person, not the company I worked for. The comments, texts, emails, and messages told me I was respected and valuable, that people trusted me and believed in me. Not just any people, but people whom I have the same respect for and feel the same way about. None of the posted comments called me "bossy," "emotional," "abrasive," "difficult," "aggressive," or even a "bitch." It turns out that I'm an inspiring and trustworthy leader.

I thought, *if people I respect can feel this way about me, why can't I feel this way about myself?* I wish it had not taken the words of others to dispel the myths I thought about myself, but other people's impressions of me allowed me to see myself in another light. I challenge you—and myself—to find your value in yourself. You are worthy; you are enough.

I'm hoping that you dispel the myths of who you think you are, who you tell yourself you are, and who you believe others think you are, and turn them upside down and on their heads. Remember, eighty percent of what you think during any day is negative, and ninety-five percent of that is on repeat. You need to start thinking about how valuable and powerful you are.

> " You wouldn't worry so
> much about what others
> think of you if you realized
> how seldom they do. "
> –Eleanor Roosevelt

Years ago, I started collecting items: let's call them "professional keepsakes." These included a list of accomplishments, letters, and emails from clients, peers, and team members, as well as awards for my work, sales successes, inspiring quotes, and other mementos. I put most of these items into what I called my "brag box." I wanted to remind myself of all I had accomplished for myself and others.

When I am feeling down or doubting myself, and my own internal validation is lagging, I open my brag box. If I ever feel like I'm not enough or that I have impostor syndrome, I can pull it out to remind myself that I'm not only great at what I do, but I'm also making an impact. I encourage each of you to start making your own brag box by capturing the kudos you receive, the things you accomplish, and the people you impact. It is not only great for self-esteem but also good prep for whatever you decide to do in your life.

Start building your brag box now.

Get a beautiful or meaningful box. Mine is a palm frond woven box from Hawaii.

Start a Word document.

Collect the information:

- Write down all of your big accomplishments to date. For example: Exceeded sales goals by 150 percent, Company Name, Year.

- Ask for LinkedIn referrals (make a note to do this every couple of months as you work with different people on different projects).

- Start keeping all notes (emails in a folder and copied onto your Word document, and notes in your brag box).

CHAPTER 4
WHAT DO OTHER WOMEN LEADERS THINK?

listened to a news show with my husband, Mom, and stepfather, and it discussed a commercial Nike aired during the Super Bowl. It was called "So, Win." It was about women in sports. Their message was:

There's one guarantee in sport.
You'll be told you can't do it.
So, do it anyway.
You can't win.
So, win.

The interviewer called this a "zombie lie," one that persists long after it is no longer valid and that we, as a society, need to stop promoting. I normally enjoyed this interviewer, but in this situation, I was offended. He just did not get it. He couldn't; he was a man. Women having similar opportunities to men in athletics is a synonym for women having the same treatment and opportunities in all aspects of life. Only women get to say when we are being treated with fairness and equality. So, I would change the theme of that ad to:

There's one guarantee in life for women.
You'll be told you can't do it.
So, do it anyway.
You can't win.
So, win.

I hear, "But look how far women have come." Don't get me wrong; so much has improved for women, but saying it has improved is a bit silly. Improved from what, not being a man's possession, not being able to have our own bank accounts without permission from our husbands, not being able to own property, or that we get treated "equally" at work. Those are a nice start. What we need to change are the attitudes of both men and women about women. This will not happen overnight. No law can be passed to change a mindset.

Later that same day, a woman I respect posted on LinkedIn, sharing how someone offered her "personal feedback." The feedback was that she was too confrontational to be part of the project she was working on with that person. *This feedback came from a man.* Would a man ever say to another man, "You are too confrontational to do _____?" No, never. I sent her a private message and said, *"Most men do not know how to handle strong women. Do not let him win! Put your strengths and influence where you can make the biggest difference."*

The expectations placed not on what women say, but on how they say it in a professional setting, are very different from those of our counterparts. That leads to women feeling almost "watched" all the time—on edge, so to speak. Don't say "too much", it may make them bossy, abrasive, emotional, difficult, aggressive, or a bitch.

My experience felt remarkably similar to what many women leaders I have spoken to reported, but I wanted to gather real-time feedback from other #bossyleaders, so I prepared a survey and asked the group what they struggled with in their professional careers. What was most interesting were the comments and text messages they sent me, rather than the actual survey results.

"For me, it's confidence speaking up or more, so how I present my feedback or opinion. I was fortunate to learn early in my career that speaking up with unyielding passion—whether about a strategy, perspective, or idea—can sometimes be misread as being 'too emotional' or 'difficult.' I'm grateful for my experience with this, as it has helped me grow. Over the last 15 years, I've worked to refine my approach, practicing a style of listening and leading that feels true to me. Embracing a positive response and 'let's explore' language has positioned me better to navigate the dynamics of working as a woman in my current role while still making room for my authentic voice." – JT

"Impostor Syndrome in certain situations, but mostly that I'll never be able to compete with the 'Penis Parade.' McKenzie Nicholas gets credit for the term. I also want to point out that OTHER WOMEN can be part of the problem. It's not just men. But also, are you tagging us because you think we're bossy? LOL. Just kidding." – AC

"✓ Impostor Syndrome, but ALSO, I think balancing empathy versus assertiveness (not sure that's the right word) is a hard one for me. I want to make everyone happy—both employees and clients— but sometimes, I find it a struggle to stand firm on what I believe is right and how I choose to handle a situation while still empathizing and understanding another person's point of view.

Maybe that's just a general personality trait, but DON'T MAKE ME MAKE YOU FEEL BAD. 😒 " – LW

"I've flipped the script on 'bossy.' It's a way of not understanding that person's leadership style, and/or the 'bossy' person not understanding how to lead in ways that resonate. Bossy to me means a leader with ideas and who has a vision." – CS

"Advocating for myself. Too many times I said to myself, 'They know how hard I work and how valuable I am; I don't need to say anything.' I was WRONG. I needed to speak up and make sure those above me knew my worth; nobody else was going to do it for me. I still struggle with this, but I'm getting better." – DY

"Being taken seriously." – RA

"Growing what is essentially a start-up business, I don't necessarily face the same struggles as so many others in corporate environments. My greatest challenge is balancing all the demands that come with running a business and taking care of my family at the same time. As women, we are more visible in our successes and areas of development. We don't have a place to hide." – KG

"For me, GUILT. I had a realization last week that I have a weird relationship with guilt (if that's what it really is), and I believe that comes with being a woman. We are always thinking of others. What I mean is, this job is TOUGH. It's tough on every department, manager, and employee every day. Even on good days, there are a thousand moving parts, tension, and inevitable communication issues. That's just the nature of the industry. But as a business owner, I'm in a position to delegate tasks in order to focus on aspects

of the business that truly fill my cup, to the benefit of the entire company, but for some reason, when I experience true joy at work, I also feel bad about it." – LM

"To be super specific, a scenario I am often struggling with when I ask a team member for a deliverable—could be something small or large, no matter—and for some reason, they don't get it done in the parameter we give them; I find myself having a hard time revisiting the task with the team member and asking why it couldn't be achieved without feeling awkward. I have no logical reason to feel awkward; I gave good communication/follow-up, asked if there was something they needed to achieve the task, and gave ample time to complete. Why do I hesitate to reach out and ask, 'What's up, team member? Why don't we have this completed?' For context, in the past, when I've just ignored the awkward feelings, I, too, am met with 'well, she's bossy' or 'she's too demanding/intimidating'...or my favorite: 'she can be so emotional.' If my male counterparts asked this of that team member, would they call him emotional? Do men feel awkward, too? WHY DO I SECOND-GUESS MYSELF!?!?! You could put this in a category of 'confidence to speak up,' but I'm not afraid to ask; I do ask—just...why does it feel unnatural? No other parts of confrontation feel this way; for some reason, it's just this one." – KS

"The 'bossy' vs 'leader' label. Because I'm a woman, I have to change my delivery in order to avoid getting slapped with 'bossy,' 'difficult,' or 'emotional' labels. The same behaviors in some of my male counterparts get labeled with 'leader,' 'driven,' and 'confident.' It messes with your confidence, your drive, and your overall sense of who you are presenting as and who you really want to be. In 2024, I still sometimes have to give ideas to my male co-workers

to present as their own for some owners to not dismiss them without consideration simply because I'm a woman talking about maintenance or data, which have historically been male-dominated topics." – HH

"I am not sure if it is impostor syndrome, but I have been told, to my face, that I haven't 'done my time.' I don't talk about my story much because I am not sure anyone would care to hear... but I can assure you, I have done my time. Taken my lumps. Been knocked down. Kept down. Dismissed. Disrespected. Passed over or rejected. I guess that there is just an expectation that we need to work twice as hard and be happy with what someone else determines our value to be. Through personal development, I've gained perspective on this system and have worked to find my own balance. I'm doing my best to focus on building my career in ways that don't perpetuate these patterns, and create a path for the people that come after." – AK

"The best way to describe what I've experienced and observed is 'benevolent patriarchy.' Women are expected to be bold and innovative in ways that don't disrupt the status quo. We're told to 'wait our turn' and avoid causing a stir, all while maintaining a 'professional' appearance and demeanor at all times, without support for balancing motherhood in a society that doesn't materially support families. This is challenging for anyone to do well without losing one's sense of self in the process." – KF

"Being known as a feather ruffler. And if you don't use enough sugar, you're labeled condescending. Avoiding the smirk." – ML

"Cooperation and amplification. Not being seen as a threat by my main male counterparts. Maybe it is just a sales vs. marketing

thing, but that was largely my experience as I climbed the ladder in sales leadership." – IIS

The words they used in their beliefs may vary from mine, but the essence is very much the same.

Many of these women who provided feedback are part of my support system. They are kick @#$ bossy leaders and part of my Support Squad. We all need each other to have an impact and be an impact on each other.

CHAPTER 5

THE POWER OF YOUR OWN SUPPORT SQUAD

To me, a "Support Squad" is a group of individuals who know you well. They know your strengths, faults, and idiosyncrasies, yet they do not all know the same dimension of your make-up, which makes having them as a support system all the more important. It's funny—when I look at who my true Squad is, they know very little of each other, if anything at all. They are peers, past employees, old friends, new friends, and family, but they all care about me, and I deeply care about each of them. These relationships take time and effort to cultivate. Cultivation comes from building trust when you are most vulnerable.

The Support Squad is not a clique. It's a group of people who can rely on you as well, so the relationship is mutual. I use my Support Squad as a support group that I can confide in, ask for advice, or even just complain to! Your Support Squad will evolve with and around you. People who were in your Support Squad today may not be there tomorrow. Your relationship might have served its purpose (for you and them, for a season or reason). If you want to know who your Support Squad is, speak your truth and see who sticks around. That's your squad.

So, why is it important to have such a group? I conducted extensive research on this topic. Having a Support Squad should provide you with a variety of people from different backgrounds and experiences that complement yours, people who are like-minded but will still challenge you. They should hold your secrets and be non-judgmental. For women who struggle with low self-esteem, impostor syndrome, or any other self-doubting thoughts, this group is not only supportive but life-changing in so many ways.

1. Women have innate and unique emotional, societal, and life challenges that only other women can understand. They naturally have empathy while they are supporting you. These points or influences do not need to be explicitly discussed, but they naturally inform the conversation.
2. The right support group will challenge and push you to stay focused on all the things you are capable of doing, even when you are doubting yourself. Sometimes, I call the members of my Support Squad "my own personal cheerleaders." We all need one of those every once in a while.
3. Being able to be real and vulnerable without fear of judgment or having a possible breach of confidence is probably the most important indicator of a true support squad. You would hope that every person on your Support Squad is someone who will not judge. I'd like to believe that I could expect this from my entire squad, but because each relationship is founded on different experiences we have together, I do not share all of my struggles with each person. I also pick and choose based on the support or help I need at the time.
4. Being a strong woman leader can be a lonely experience. There are not a lot of us, and some women leaders are not

supportive of other women leaders. So, having another strong woman leader who also supports you is a real blessing.

5. Sometimes, we don't take credit or acknowledge our accomplishments, but a great Support Squad *won't let you ignore your success*. They'll tell you just how amazing you are and celebrate your wins, no matter how small. Having a strong circle of supportive women is like having an emotional safety net. It's about sisterhood, shared wisdom, and lifting each other up in a world that sometimes tries to wear and tear us down.

In my long career (and life), I have relied on my Support Squad more times than I can count. When I'm feeling down or need a pick-me-up, I run through the people in my squad and select the one with the best experience or background relevant to the problem I'm facing (personal or professional).

At one time, I was fortunate enough to have my company invest in a 360-degree review of me as a peer to the leadership group I worked with. When it came back, there were comments and findings that I questioned and disagreed with. I felt like some individuals were being unjustly harsh. I was in a quandary about what to do with the information to improve myself.

It took all the courage I had to share the 360 review with a member of my Support Squad. Talk about vulnerability. This person was also a client of mine, someone I trusted and had a great amount of respect for. The feedback and advice they provided gave me solid takeaways and actionable steps in areas where I could improve my behaviors and communication style. I could not have been more open to the feedback because I trusted him. We developed a plan of execution, which significantly changed how I communicated and worked with my teams. At the next major offsite I attended, I felt significantly better about my role and my team.

SEASON, REASON, OR LIFETIME

My mom always said to me, "People will be in your life for a reason, season, or a lifetime." None of these are bad, and if they're in your life for a reason or season, it does not mean the relationship will end; it just means it has served its purpose. It isn't easy, however, to acknowledge when someone in your Support Squad moves on because a season or reason has ended.

I had been struggling in a relationship I had with another strong woman in leadership. She and I had exchanged cross-mentoring positions for years, depending on which of us needed support and where. All of a sudden, all communication was cut off. I was heartbroken to lose a Support Squad member, but also confused, so I reached out to another woman in my Support Squad who knew us both well. I provided her with some background information, and her feedback was genuine, meaningful, and precise.

I took her advice and decided that my relationship with that person had served its purpose, that the lack of communication was a defensive mechanism she needed for some reason. This was not about me; it was about her. I told myself, *Stop taking things personally, Michelle. Let the relationship have its natural ending. Let go of control.* This is a lesson I have learned too many times, but without my Support Squad, I would still be wondering, *What did I do wrong?* The answer is nothing. The season or reason had just changed. Realizing this, I changed from feeling resentful to empowered.

As you grow in leadership and maturity, there will be times when you might have to decide that people you care about are not acting in a way that also values you, and that it is time to end the depth of that relationship.

Think about all the stages you go through in life and the support you might need:

- *Single and career-focused.*
- *Married and balancing the expectations of your husband, the community, and your employer.*
- *A working mom, struggling to decide which comes first, career or family?*
- *An inspiring leader, wondering how to balance it all.*

At every stage of your life, your support squad may subtly change to accommodate your needs and their needs. That is okay. Remember, you can still have a relationship with them; it just changes over time. It is impossible to have a LARGE, sincere support squad. There are too many relationships to invest in.

Pay attention when a season or reason is up. Know that it is okay to surround yourself with people who truly understand you and learn from those who do not. I also try to think about the "season, reason, lifetime," and how I fit into other people's lives. Rarely do I interact with people I will be involved with for a lifetime, but I do want to positively and meaningfully influence the people I spend time with.

Have you ever had someone call you for advice or support, and you think, *Oh, gosh, I don't have time for that now?* Then you dread calling them back? We have all experienced something like that. I ask myself, *Am I one of those people?* How do we know we are building up a strong relationship with someone?

One of my favorite authors and researchers, Brené Brown, shared a story about her daughter in a 2015 speech on how to build meaningful relationships. Here is a transcript of the speech:

"One day, my daughter, Ellen, came home from school. She was in third grade. And the minute we closed the front door, she literally just started sobbing and slid down the door until she was just kind of a heap of crying on the floor. And of course I was... It scared me, and I said, "What's wrong, Ellen? What happened? What happened?"

And she pulled herself together enough to say, "Something really hard happened to me today at school, and I shared it with a couple of my friends during recess. And by the time we got back into the classroom, everyone in my class knew what had happened, and they were laughing and pointing at me and calling me names." And it was so bad, and the kids were being so disruptive, that her teacher even had to take marbles out of this marble jar.

And the marble jar in the classroom is a jar where, if the kids are making great choices together, the teacher adds marbles. If they're making not-great choices, the teacher takes out marbles. And if the jar gets filled up, there's a celebration for the class.

And so, she said, "It was one of the worst moments in my life. They were laughing and pointing. And Miss Bacchum, my teacher, kept saying, 'I'm going to take marbles out.' And she didn't know what was happening."

And she looked at me just with this face that just seared my mind and said, "I will never trust anyone again." And my first reaction, to be really honest with you, was, "Damn straight. You don't tell anybody anything but your mama."

Yeah, right? That's it. I mean, that was my... "You just tell me. And when you grow up and you go off to school, Mama will go, too. I'll get a little apartment." And the other thing I was thinking, to be quite honest with you, is, "I will find out who those kids were." And while I'm not going to beat up a nine-year-old, I know their mamas.

You know, that's the place you go to. And I'm like, "How am I going to explain trust to this third-grader in front of me?" So, I took a deep breath, and I said, "Ellen, trust is like a marble jar." She said, "What do you mean?" And I said, "You share those hard stories and those hard things that are happening to you with friends, who, over time, you filled up their marble jar. They've done thing after thing after thing where you're like, 'I know I can share this with this person.' Does that make sense?"

Yes!

And that's what Ellen said, "Yes, that makes sense." And I said, "Do you have any marble jar friends?" And she said, "Oh, yeah. Totally. Hannah and Lorna are marble jar friends." And I said... and then this is where things got interesting. I said, "Tell me what you mean. How do they earn marbles for you?"

And she's like, "Well, Lorna, if there's not a seat for me at the lunch cafeteria, she'll scoot over and give me half a heinie seat." And I'm like, "She will?" She's like, "Yeah. She'll just sit like that, and so I can sit with her." And I said, "That's a big deal." This is not what I was expecting to hear.

And then she said, "And you know Hannah, on Sunday at my soccer game?" And I was waiting for this story, where she said, "I got hit by a ball, and I was lying on the field, and Hannah picked me up and ran me to first aid." And I was like, "Yeah?" And she said, "Hannah looked over and she saw Oma and Opa, my parents, her grandparents, and she said, 'Look, your Oma and Opa are here.'"

And I was like, "Boy, she got a marble for that?" And she goes, "Well, you know, not all my friends have eight grandparents." Because my parents are divorced and remarried, my husband's parents were divorced and remarried. And she said, "And it was so nice to me that she remembered their names."

And I was like, "Hmm." And she said, "Do you have marble jar friends?" And I said, "Yeah, I do have a couple of marble jar friends." And she said, "Well, what kind of things do they do to get marbles?" And this feeling came over me. And I thought... The first thing I could think of, because we were talking about the soccer game, was that same game. My good friend Eileen walked up to my parents and said, "Diane, David, good to see you." And I remember what that felt like for me. And I was like, certainly, trust cannot be built by these small, insignificant moments in our lives. It's gotta be a grander gesture than that.

*So, as a researcher, I start looking into the data. I gather up the doctoral students who've worked with me. We start looking. And it is crystal clear. **Trust is built in very small moments.** And when we started looking at examples of when people talked about trust in the research, they said things like, "Yeah, I really trust my boss. She even asked me how my mom's chemotherapy was going."*

*"I trust my neighbor because if something's going on with my kid.
It doesn't matter what she's doing. She'll come over and help me,
FIO." You know, one of the number one things that emerged
around trust and small things? People who attend funerals. "This
is someone who showed up at my sister's funeral."*
FIO–Brené Brown, 2015

I have used a similar theory over the years. I call it "depositing into the
friendship bank." You must deposit into the bank through small but
meaningful ways, and then you can withdraw when you need something.
But if you are constantly withdrawing (asking for favors, leaning on
them, expecting more than you give, talking only about yourself) from
your relationship bank, you will find in time that the bank is bankrupt.
There is nothing more to take. The friendship fades away. I have had
friends (and fleeting members of my Support Squad) who withdrew far
more than they deposited into our relationship bank, and those relationships changed over time. And that is okay. A season, a reason, or a
lifetime.

I try to deposit into my squad by being a member of their squads.
They might not even know or understand that they have a squad, but I
strive to be available and consistently supportive in small and big ways.
You might even take the time to understand how they feel love or appre-
ciation, so your deposits make a meaningful impact. *The 5 Languages of
Appreciation in the Workplace* is a great book on that topic.

My squad includes two bossy leaders in my daughters, Sienna and
Mikala. Both give me feedback with gentleness because they know I am
sensitive, which I appreciate. Sometimes, I think, *How are they so smart
about such grown-up things?*

My best friend, Christi, listens to my stories over and over, whether
they're about work or personal drama. Her advice is always selfless. We've
been friends since I was fourteen and she was sixteen. She is so much

older than I am (inside joke). She gives me truthful information in the kindest, most "hearable" way, and that is something I value most about our relationship.

I have a few men in my squad as well: number one of those men is my husband. Many years ago, he started a tradition with me. When I was on my way out to what I called "a big-girl meeting" (this is what I called my meetings when I was early in my career and still trying to find my way in leadership), he stood tall, put his shoulders back, stuck his chest out, and called out to me, "Head up, chest out, kick ass, and don't let them push you around." He now says that whenever I have an important meeting. He is unwavering in his support of me and has been a leader in my Support Squad for over forty years.

Other men have also been part of my Support Squad. They know me well, both professionally and personally, so their feedback and advice are always highly relevant. People I have led or mentored over time (both men and women) have become part of my squad. They lift me up when I need it, and we support each other. I have ended up with men and women who have been my personal raving fans. I have a small but powerful group of peers, and they don't buy the false personas that follow me or other women leaders. They don't believe any of the usual assumptions of who I am: aggressive, assertive, bitchy. Surround yourself with those people.

Here is an important point about your squad: would the people in your squad name you as a member of theirs? If not, up your game. (It's all about those marbles.) My Support Squad has evolved over time, and yours will, too!

I Challenge You: Name your Support Squad. Who is in your Support Squad? Are you nurturing those valuable relationships? How? Be intentional. It might just be a quick text!

Five ways to deposit into your Support Squad:

1. If you know something about a recent success they had, post about it on LinkedIn.

2. If you see them do something worthy of bragging, send a note to their boss. I recently saw a leader at another company in action (she is not part of my squad, but I wanted to lift her up), and I texted her to share how impressed I was with what I had seen. I also sent the COO a text sharing how well this person shone and how well she represented the company.

3. Send a little gift. I send books as my favorite go-to, such as leadership books I have loved. I will write a note on the inside of the book, sharing what I got out of it and why I sent it to them.

4. Send a note. A handwritten note goes a long way, and very few people do it anymore.

5. Introduce them to someone who could help them or their business.

CHAPTER 6
IS THERE ROOM FOR MORE WOMEN IN LEADERSHIP?

hen I conducted the survey I mentioned earlier in the book, I received quite a bit of feedback about how women can be unsupportive of other women. I have always felt that women can be both the best and the worst in supporting each other, so that information was not a surprise to me.

I heard a speaker once say, "Ladies, this is not a pie that only has so many pieces. We can just make the pie larger and make room for more of us." With so many obstacles preventing women from achieving equality in leadership, I wish we could all recognize our role in the lack of growth for women in leadership. I have personally witnessed this behavior in action. I probably participated in the behavior at one time or another. Society tells us there are limited roles for women, so we start to believe it.

I remember a time when I was interviewing for a role and called to get a reference from someone I knew who was also familiar with the company I was interviewing with. He gave me some good feedback, but one of the things that stood out was this comment: "You should take it quickly, while they are looking for diversity and wanting to hire a woman."

He was serious. Was I a DEI hire? I thought, *So he thinks the role is available to me, not because I am qualified, but because they need a woman.*

I took the job, but I knew I would be working in an organization with few female leaders. Such experiences are likely part of the reason women perceive leadership roles as scarce and precious, and that only a select few will be given the opportunity.

There have even been times when I thought people were part of my "squad," only to learn they looked at women's success as something scarce and finite. I want to mention that this has happened to me more than once, both professionally and personally, and it hurts. Such women believe that there's an expiration date on success, that you only get so much of it and then it's somebody else's turn. They then just pull each other down, like we are all crabs trapped in a bucket.

I was at a conference (a women's conference!) a few years ago, and I felt that a vibe had changed with a group of women in leadership whom I liked and respected. It was clear that something was going on. I felt like an outsider (like in high school), and it sent me into a downward spiral in my confidence and happiness. Later, during the same conference, someone told me that this same group had said some unkind things about me, repeating and spreading a rumor about me.

I am sure many of us have been the person talked about or the group talking. If I cared less about what people thought of me, I might have let this go, but we were at a women's conference, and if I was on their agenda, so were other women. Weren't we all there to be positive about women in leadership?

So, I decided to address it. I worked up the courage to ask one of the women to take a bit of time with me. After I shared what I had heard, she admitted to being involved with the conversation. I asked her if she had ever seen any of the behavior from me that she had described in that conversation. "No," she said. "I haven't." I then asked if she could do me a simple favor: could she refrain from repeating things she did not have firsthand experience with? She looked at me and she said, "You're right. I shouldn't have done that," and she apologized. We had a shot of tequila and then moved on to what I hope is a better relationship.

Don't judge a book by what another person says; decide for yourself once you have firsthand knowledge. As a group, women tend to pull each other down, and when we do that, we actually pull us all down. The talk erodes trust, not just in the person being discussed, but other women in the room also take notice and know they cannot trust that group. Over time, this leads to an erosion of trust in some of the strongest leaders we will know.

Recently, one of my mentees shared that she was working with another woman who was acting passively-aggressively, making work difficult for both of them. She wanted advice on how to handle it. I advised her to have a direct conversation, but to start by asking questions about how she could help the other person: "Look to help and give as much as possible, and in the end, she will want to give. You know, deposit into that bank." It worked!

"Real queens fix each other's crowns. And they don't tell the world it was crooked"

When I met my most recent coach, Amber, I was sitting at a table at a conference, getting ready to speak. I'd had a harrowing morning and was a bit frazzled. We knew "of" each other but had never met. We chit-chatted at breakfast, and I got up to go behind the stage before speaking. All of a sudden, she was there and said, "Hang on, honey." After fixing my hair and giving me some lipstick, she said, "We lady leaders need to stick together." I knew immediately that I wanted to work with her. She fixed my crown before I went out onto that stage.

So many of us love having conversations with conflict, right? So, how do you have a productive conversation with a woman you are having conflict with?

How to Have Difficult Conversations with Women in Leadership

1. Set aside time. Do not try to talk about the situation as part of another topic.

2. Face-to-face for all confrontational conversations if possible. Zoom if not, with cameras on.

3. Start with the end in mind. Do you want to be right, or do you want a stronger relationship? Do not start the conversation without being sure about what you want the outcome to be. Even write it down before the call.

4. Start with your goal for the conversation. State specifically what you hope to accomplish.

5. Be sincere.

6. Before the call, ask yourself, I feel _____ when [X] happens; is there a way we can talk about that?

7. Ask a lot of questions: "Our communication has felt strained. What can I do to make this easier for us?"

8. Build them up: "You are strong in [XYZ], while I struggle with those areas. Could you help me with _____? I would really appreciate it."

9. Give kudos publicly and often: "_____ and I worked on [X] project, and without her experience in [XYZ], it would not have been as successful."

If we bring one of us down, do the rest of us get an advantage? Does making other women look bad make the rest of us look good? ***Here is what I think.*** It is so f#@$ing hard to get into leadership roles, and when we do get there, we are playing defense for the role/position/influence/authority. Do we feel like only one woman can shine? Are we so entrenched with our own self-talk that we can't be empathetic, understanding that we share the same plight? Could they, too, have beliefs that are holding them back and need your help to overcome the societal judgment that has consumed their minds? We have all heard about the idea of paying it forward. I would love it if we could just do that. #womenwhopayitforward

I challenge you. Is there a woman you work with in any capacity with whom you struggle? Ask yourself, What are her strengths vs. my weaker areas? Ask for her support in the area in which she could help you. Use what she gives you and share the results. Share the results not just with her but loudly and proudly to her boss or in front of a group of people. Acknowledge how her advice allowed you to succeed. She might just surprise you and ask for your help with something.

CHAPTER 7
GENDER BIASED BELIEFS

n this chapter, I will share with you the seven beliefs (and biased perceptions that I and others have had about women leaders) that have consistently contributed to my self-doubts and opinions of myself throughout my life. As Dr Schawn Andrews says in her TED talk:

"Men are socialized to be confident and assertive, while women are socialized to be empathetic and skilled at relationships, even if we are not naturally inclined that way. The results of this mean we put pressure on male leaders to be confident, strong, not vulnerable, and not show emotion. We put pressure on our female leaders to be supportive, collaborative, and social. What would happen if we did not look at male and female societal stereotypes? How would our companies be different? How would our society be different? How would our world be different?

The data points to higher performance, job satisfaction, higher employee engagement, and more equal representation in our leadership positions."
– Dr. Schawn Andrews, Breaking Bias: Leadership Lessons from the Workplace, TEDx talk, December 2018

For example, I had a couple of situations where I worked with a team of mostly men. They were all close, and I was the outsider. Instead of trying to be part of their "insiders" club, I decided that being professional and taking the high road would be the way to behave. In both examples, the team would travel somewhere together, and my boss would come back with "feedback" about my performance, attitude, or relationship, all based on what he had heard from the gossiping men.

At first, I was defensive (he had only heard one side), but he told me I was being sensitive. I decided that I needed to share more of my experiences with my peers with that same leader. I was then told to go to work it out with them directly, and that he did not want to hear about our communication or accountability issues. So, I went back to the high road. I worked tirelessly on the relationship and never shared additional feedback with the CEO.

Here is what happened. That other male continued feeding the leader false information about what I was doing or not doing, and the CEO believed everything he heard. I was absent from the conversation, and in the end, I was the odd man out. I should have been at the table in those conversations. I wish I had stuck up for myself. I learned a difficult lesson. Staying quiet worked against me. I believe to this day that he saw my feedback as whining and took my male counterpart's feedback as fact, and it was given a heavy weight to this leader's opinion of me and the job I was going for. Women will NEVER be in the "boys club."

As you can see from the quotes from the #bossyleaders earlier in this book, my self-beliefs are typical of those felt by many women, particularly strong women in leadership positions. As you read through the behaviors, ask yourself, *Would anyone ever call a man any of these words?* They are reserved for strong women leaders who do not conform to a societal mold of how women are expected to behave.

CHAPTER 8
BEHIND THE MASK

As I mentioned, writing what I believed was "behind the mask" was not very flattering to someone who has not only been successful but also a good leader of other people. What was behind the words and the deep introspection is what becomes interesting in my self-reflection.

I am aware that many of these beliefs have hindered both my development as a leader and my career advancement. I still act/do things the way society "thinks" I should rather than listening to my intuition or acting on my natural instinct. Yes, work in progress.

OWNING YOUR LEADERSHIP: WHY "BOSSY" IS A STRENGTH, NOT A FLAW

Every report card I ever received described me as both talkative and bossy. Most women I know, including my mom, my daughters, and female colleagues, have had this belief attributed to them. When I have been called bossy, it has always been in a derogatory way.

When you read descriptions of women being bossy in leadership, you see words like "decisive," "authoritative," "tough," "direct," and "has high expectations." Personally, I think it has been about setting clear expectations and challenging the status quo. When I read the words above, I thought, *Yes, I am bossy. So, why is that bad?* Because society says it is. This comes back to the societal expectations of women being collaborative and supportive, rather than any of the complimentary descriptions above. It comes as a surprise when a woman leader behaves like a man (direct, decisive, tough), and therefore, words like "bossy" are used. When our male counterparts are described, they are not called "bossy" but "strong leaders."

For me, being "bossy" was about being able to control the outcomes of a project or department I led with clarity. There was a better chance of success if everyone was aligned and clear about the objectives, including who, when, and how we would all commit to specific pieces of any project or business plan.

I ask myself, *How do we reframe the inner critic's voice to see that being bossy is actually a strong leadership style?* We cannot take on societal norms with just this one book, but we can control how we refer to the women we raise, lead, or mentor. I have already started this with my daughters, granddaughters, and the women I work with or mentor.

Being "bossy" has served me well. When people work with me, they know that I am reliable when it comes to being strategic on the project, but also that I'm willing to dig into the details. *Bossy* has helped me feel confident about leading just about anything. I am also skilled enough to know that I am not an expert at everything, so being bossy also means knowing where my weaknesses are and filling those gaps with other team members.

I think that a strong woman should feel confident about taking charge, and let's flip that adjective from negative to positive. When you are bossy, you're a strong leader, and that's powerful. For those of you who are called bossy, think about it differently. Own it. Being bossy is not a flaw but a strength!

"I'm not bossy. I am confident in my ability to lead."

HOW TO BE CANDID WITHOUT BEING LABELED ABRASIVE

When I was nineteen, I told my mom that I was going to take a semester off from attending college. Let's not call it "attending" because I scheduled my school hours around tequila Tuesdays and tanning hours. Fun was important! I met a boy while I was "attending" school who had moved to the island of Maui. He invited me to move there, so without giving it much thought, I bought a one-way ticket and moved to Maui. I packed everything I would need and left everything else behind, including a car packed with belongings in an alley in San Diego. This was very irresponsible of me—and very brave, looking back. I had $80 (equivalent to $253 today) in my pocket and an uncashed paycheck for about the same amount.

At that time, the airport on the west side of Maui was very small, and the planes landing were six-seaters, with one of the seats, the jump seat, next to the pilot. I landed on this small airstrip located along the ocean. It was not much of an airport, just a bar called the Windsock on the second story of a very small building. The trade winds were blowing hard from the ocean through the kiawe trees.

As everyone disembarked the plane and either were picked up or drove away in their rental cars, I just stood there with my five small bags filled with everything I owned, looking very lost. Even the plane was gone. There was no sign of the boy I had followed to Maui. That was the first time I thought, *What was I thinking?* The boy I followed did not have a landline phone and there were no cell phones.

I called a friend of his who did have a phone and said, "Hi, Brian. This is Michelle, Kirk-o's girlfriend. I am at the airport. Do you know where he is?" Long story short, he sent a cab to come get me and take me to what was called the "solstice pad." The friend of his I called is now my husband of over thirty-seven years, Brian. Now, that is a whole other story for another time. When I got to the solstice pad, the boy I was moving in with was just pulling up with his surfboard on his friend's car and said, "Oh, dude, is it the twenty-first?" He had completely forgotten I was coming.

Living on Maui was expensive and I worked three jobs (renting jet skis on the beach, waitressing, and cleaning houses) before I found my first "real job." That job was selling activities and tours on Front Street in Lahaina. I had never done sales before, but selling activities sounded fun. There was a man named Nick there. He was a satire of his nickname, Nick the Greek (open shirt with hairy chest and a thick gold chain), and the number one salesperson that everybody wanted to beat.

Within the first month, I did beat him. I beat him in the second month and then beat him in the third month. I was quickly number one in sales. Selling was easy for me. I had long ago understood what commission selling (waitressing is commission selling) meant and how to encourage people to spend more money with me. The "way" I sold was something I knew I could teach other people. I started pitching myself to the company I worked for as a sales manager. The owners were not buying it, but I also noticed that the company was disorganized, with no procedures or policies in place to ensure things ran more smoothly. It was clear to me that the owners were frustrated with this.

I convinced the company owners to hire me on an hourly basis to document (type) how things were supposed to run, which was probably the most expensive typing job anyone has ever been hired for. Did I mention the only bad grade I ever got, which ruined my GPA, was in typing? It began with typing out an employee list, but it quickly grew.

Long story short, I was promoted to sales manager and later to general manager. I ended up, at twenty-four years old, running the entire business. I grew the company's revenue from $3 million to $10 million within a couple of years. I knew I was doing a good job based on the overall growth the company was seeing.

But one day, the owners took me out to lunch, and I excitedly awaited the kudos I was sure to receive—and maybe even a raise. Instead, they critiqued my approach to employees. They said to me, "It's not what you say; it's how you say it." I was direct (bossy) in how I communicated, and did not have any experience in how to hold people accountable and have conversations without just being direct. No softening statements, no cushioning, no "sandwiching."

My mom had always told me, "Don't say anything behind someone's back unless you would say it to their face." I think I had taken this literally. I made sure that instead of saying something behind their back, I said it directly to their faces. The owners shared feedback with me that my abrasiveness was pissing people off. I was so focused on doing the job and achieving results that I hadn't given enough consideration to the people I led. My stomach turned, and I felt sick. Was I going to be fired?

No, they were lovely people who wanted to invest in me even further. What they did was hire a mentor for me. Her name was Cotty, and we're gonna have an entire chapter about mentorship because I believe it's so important. Cotty taught me so much, and I will forever be grateful to her. One of the areas of focus for us was on how to communicate with authority and accountability to peers and team members without coming across as abrasive (men are not typically perceived as abrasive, by the way).

Over the years, I learned how to have direct conversations and get buy-in or agreement to adjust our expectations of the plan or situation. I was so successful at having direct but constructive conversations with customers that one employer said to me, "Michelle, you could tell someone their baby was ugly, and they would say, 'Thank you.'" This was his way of saying that I could deliver bad news without hurting relationships.

That same boss once texted me, "Hey, Michelle, I want you to read two books: *Leading with Luv* and *Getting Naked*."

I laughed and said, "Do I need to call HR?"

Leading with Luv explores the concept of leadership based on "love," essentially prioritizing people and treating employees and customers with care and respect. It demonstrates that a genuine focus on human connection can lead to exceptional business success, even in a competitive market.

Getting Naked is all about being candid, direct, and telling the truth, even if that means you might lose a customer. This book concludes that you want to have such direct conversations with your partners that you don't hold anything back, yet remain kind.

These two books helped me refine my communication with others. I still believe that being direct is important, but it is also important to approach people with kindness and diplomacy. The book was very aligned with how I tried to communicate with customers and team members, and after reading it, I used it to share my style. This allowed me to be direct because I could share the book and ask for permission to be candid.

At a pivotal point in my career, I was presenting to a large and important client. I had all the C-level executives around the table. I'd brought the book *Getting Naked*, and I had highlighted areas that I believed were important. I began by explaining why I had brought the book and how I hoped to have a candid and direct conversation. I said, "This conversation may not be comfortable for you or me, but in the end, I think it'll make for a better meeting and attain a better outcome. Is everyone comfortable with that?" The meeting was tough for everyone at the table.

I shared what I had seen in their business that the group had been a little blind to.

A few days later, my boss asked me to come to his office and said, "Michelle, I got a call from [client]." He shared that I had ruffled a few feathers in the meeting. Then he added, "But he [the client] also wants you to be in every strategic meeting they have with us because he thinks they are better with you there."

"I am not abrasive. I'm candid, and I'm a truth-teller.
Candor with kindness is possible!"

EMOTIONS AS A LEADERSHIP STRENGTH: HOW TO HARNESS PASSION WITHOUT LOSING CREDIBILITY

Throughout my life, I have been told I am sensitive and emotional. There are pieces of me that think that's true. However, I believe this is more about the way in which women show their emotions—or, for me, how my frustrations show through emotion. In my experience, in the workplace, men are often free to express emotions, which typically manifest as anger.

Meanwhile, if I—or any other woman leader—were to be angry or tear up during a meeting, it would be interpreted in one of two ways: that we are a bitches or too sensitive. Either way, people would say, "She is too emotional."

While I am aware of the stigma that men have placed on women as being "too emotional," I have found in my time that the same stigma is not applied to men. I remember being in meetings where I watched the chins of my male colleagues quiver from holding back tears. The men who teared up would be taken seriously, and then the topic of discussion would be of higher priority, almost as if it were more serious.

My biggest problem is that I tend to be "emotional" when I am frustrated or angry, when I am unable to get a message across, or when I feel like somebody is being unreasonable. Throughout my time in the workforce, I have learned to manage my emotions effectively. Otherwise, I would not be taken seriously, and people (men) would lose respect. Frustration, for me, comes from caring about the results of conversations.

As you know, "emotional" is not a word people generally use to describe a good leader. In my opinion, however, the emotional aspect is what allows me to find passion in work, because I truly care about what I am doing.

> *"I am not emotional. I am invested,*
> *and I care deeply."*

HOW TO OWN BEING "DIFFICULT" WITHOUT FEELING GUILTY

I held a sales role where I consistently exceeded my goals by 400 percent. That meant a big bonus for me! The director of sales called me into his office and asked me to sit across from him. There were two chairs in front of his desk. I sat in one, and he sat in the other. He moved the chairs (while I was sitting in one) to face each other and inched them closer together.

After talking about the great quarter I'd had, he then went on to "mansplain" why he could not possibly pay out my bonus. He shared that they had never thought anyone would exceed their targets as much as I had. He then put his hand on my leg and said, "You are one of the smart ones. You understand why we couldn't pay out that much money and why others wouldn't." Then he got up and opened the door for me to leave.

I was shocked. Around that same time, that same director of sales asked me to cheat on an expense form (cash had been advanced to me for a sales trip we took together) by creating fake receipts for the cash. In both scenarios, I was torn between going with the flow and not causing trouble or being seen as difficult. Integrity is a pillar to me, and after careful consideration, I decided to share the situation with human resources.

Later, at an all-team sales meeting, he shared with everyone (including me) that someone in our "family" had gone to HR and disclosed some "family" problems, as well as how that person had undermined the team he was trying to build. He went on to say this person was clearly difficult and not part of this team. He quietly bullied me until I quit my job. In my exit interview, I shared all of my experiences.

I've never been very good at politicking—you know, where one-on-one meetings occur before the main meeting to discuss the topic and preferred outcome, and then those individuals meet with the main group to inform them of what they've already decided. There were times when I would enter a meeting, ready to discuss the topic at hand. I would get pushback on just about anything I brought up, only to find out that a decision had already been made. So, I just appeared to be difficult to the group. I would back down on speaking up because I did not want to appear difficult, but then I left the meeting feeling guilty for not giving it my call.

I also found that when the politicking is going on, there is usually chatter amongst the team or discussion at what I call "the meetings *after* the meeting." In many of these situations, I would find out that those individuals didn't actually support the topic or outcome but felt like they had to go along, like they were almost bullied. Maybe "bullied" is not the word, but they were strongly encouraged by other leaders to take a stance that they didn't believe in, without sharing their concerns in the meeting itself.

Again, I could have just gone with the flow, but I also found myself a cheerleader of underdogs (people or situations). If somebody is being treated unfairly, I am not afraid to have a hard, direct conversation. This might make others think I'm a contrarian. But I'm a leader who is passionate about what I do, and it's important that I speak up for what I believe is right for the business. I also lean toward supporting employees and customers. I can't help but cheer for the underdog. It's just something in me. This means, at meetings, I will bring things up that other people will not say because they're afraid to. Then I come across as difficult or hard to manage.

When women push against the status quo, they challenge other leaders to do the same. It is a superpower of mine to identify areas for improvement and bring those things forward. For other leaders, this could feel threatening (especially when society expects women to be demure and agreeable) and difficult.

Are there times that it makes sense just to go with the flow, or not come across as difficult? How do you know when something is important enough to fight for? My line in the sand is ethical items, large-scale strategies that would affect the client or employees, and anyone being bullied, even if it is me.

Don't be afraid to be difficult (challenge the status quo or hold people accountable to agreed-upon outcomes). Just be sure to check your motives. If they are not rooted in truth or if there is even a hint of competitiveness or a breakdown in a relationship, take a beat before you act.

"I am not difficult. I speak the truth, challenge the status quo, and hold people accountable to their words and actions."

WHY WOMEN LEADERS NEED TO BE AGGRESSIVE, NOT APOLOGETIC

At one point in my career, I was attending an offsite with our executive team where we focused on the issue of missing multiple objectives for the year, and a few things that were happening that we wanted to solve for, like high employee turnover, high customer churn, and missing roadmap deadlines.

In general, the team was very focused on evaluating and updating processes around hiring, training, alignment, procedures, documentation, and communication. We were single-mindedly focused on solutions, but we had not identified the root cause of the problem. I believed, however, that a majority of our problems could be solved by addressing the negative culture that had been created at the company. I felt that the company had constructed a culture where employees were told what to do and were not involved in identifying problems or asked how they would solve them. Consequently, they felt undervalued and unheard. They were then less engaged in meeting the objectives. They were completing one piece of the puzzle without seeing what the entire puzzle looked like. Have you ever tried that? It isn't easy. This led to employees feeling isolated and disconnected from a larger purpose.

At this meeting, I was like a dog with a bone. I just kept saying, "This is not a process problem. This is a people problem."

The group responded, "Then we need to hire new people."

They still were not getting it. I shared: "People want to know you care. It's about how they feel about going to work every day."

My fellow C-suite members were so process-oriented that it took a while for them to be convinced. There were people there who thought I was aggressive, difficult, and stubborn when it came to sticking to my talk track.

Finally, people began to understand. As easy as I make this sound, it was not like the flick of a switch after they understood the problem. We still had to build a system to change the culture, bring in experts, and involve fellow team members who were well aware of the issues and how to address them.

As a woman, when you do get a seat at that table, you come to it as an underdog. You do not instantly know what you are supposed to do. Every organization has its own norms and customs. Add the fact that you're one of maybe two women (if you are lucky), and you have to almost "own" the spot. You have to *"earn* it until you *learn* it, and you have to push yourself into the agenda, into the conversations, because they're not typically going to invite you in.

I have been talked over. I have had men roll their eyes in front of me and behind my back. I've been bullied at meetings. I have had men take my ideas and present them as their own. I have learned that I need to have tough skin and be ready to use aggression—let's call it assertiveness—though that is not how society typically views this behavior in women leaders. In the end, *you have to stand your ground.*

Why does all of this happen? I don't know. It might be that men and some women truly don't know how to handle women they see as difficult and aggressive. They have biases that they don't even know they have. I believe that when some people run into strong women leaders, one of whom I consider myself to be, they just don't even know how to handle a strong, self-confident (outside, of course) woman sharing her firm opinions. When a woman is aggressive in a meeting, the observation is that "she's a bitch," "she's difficult," or "she's aggressive" because that's how some people innately see women leaders.

One thing to take away is that, in my experience, leading is not a popularity contest. There are times when leaders have to be aggressive and assertive to get shit done. A lot of hard decisions have to be made when you're leading, and you have to really take ownership and push through, even when you don't want to. But I can tell you that I have had to fire people who have then come back to me and said, "Thank you. You were way ahead of your time, and you taught me things that I now use every day, and I get it." I feel proud that I have been able to lead in a way that encourages people to grow and develop.

"I am not aggressive. I push for resolution.
I push for accountability."

CONFIDENCE VS. INTIMIDATING: THE FINE LINE WOMEN LEADERS WALK

The first time someone told me they were intimidated by me, I was shocked. I thought, *Wow, my persona out there is way different than who I see myself as.* I started to ask people I trusted about that. One person, for whom I have a great amount of respect and admiration, told me that I valued results over people. I thought , *Ouch. Is that true?* So, I thought about that.

I'm not sure if I value results more than people, but I certainly will let people know what I expect of them and then assume they'll deliver on that unless they tell me otherwise. It's essential to me to share my expectations clearly and then be willing to have the crucial conversation (as described in *Crucial Conversations*, a valuable book) with them about not meeting the agreed-upon outcomes. I am not afraid to have those difficult conversations, and I think that can be scary for people.

I once had a salesperson who was not meeting any of his sales goals. When I dug in, he was not even doing any of the basics. His résumé had been overflowing with great experience, and he had even been a sales manager. After many conversations spent trying to get him to the place he needed to be without success, I asked him, "What would you do if you were me?"

He said, "I probably would give myself another month." Remember, this was after several conversations had taken place.

I agreed to give him more time, one day at a time. "If you change your behavior tomorrow, you get to stay until Monday. If your activity level is still as we have agreed by Monday, then you can stay until Tuesday, and so on."

On Friday, he failed to complete any of the necessary activities. We met at the end of the day, and he convinced me to give him until the end of the day on Monday to show he was serious about turning around his performance. I let him go at the end of the day on Monday. He shared with human resources that I was intimidating. I felt like we had a very clear conversation about my expectations, and he agreed to them. However, he didn't deliver on any of his promises.

There is such a balance between being intimidating (strong and unafraid) and being too soft. If you are too soft or even share how hard some of these decisions are, you are emotional. You are damned if you do and damned if you don't.

As I mentioned earlier, getting a seat at the leadership table requires confidence, and not allowing people to push you around requires a bit of outward-looking confidence. So, showing you are strong from the get-go also gives you some sort of protection. Perhaps being intimidating was a coping mechanism, but in reality, it is a strength because I will not be pushed around, and I will have the confidence to speak my mind and tell the truth.

Writing this book has been eye-opening in so many ways. For example, was I intimidating because it was armor to protect myself from being pushed around? If I were scary, would it keep people at bay? I recall that being a "bully" in high school was about protecting myself from being hurt by others. However, in the end, it has served me well because I am not afraid to speak my mind and express the truth.

"I am not intimidating. I will not be bullied.
I will speak the truth."

FROM BITCH TO BOSS: TAKING BACK THE NARRATIVE

The word "bitch" is used almost as a weapon, a way to be derogatory and quickly categorize a woman as someone who is purposely mean or wants to hurt others. It has no place in the professional world. Women are given this label primarily by other women. I know that I have been called a bitch many times and have also called other women the same (even in professional meetings).

Why did I use that word? To be hurtful. When I reflected on this situation, I realized that I was feeling frustrated and unsure about the person's behavior. Why didn't I say, "I am confused over this conversation, and it feels personal. Can you and I talk privately about this?" That is the grown-up way to handle such situations. That is real leadership, but such growth takes reflection.

I thought that if I came across as confident, strong, and direct, people would not question me or my abilities or skills. I have had to show strength in everything (from literally being beaten up at school to being chased down an alley by a gang of boys or being in positions I was not ready for), and I have had to come across as *strong*, with an air of "don't mess with me."

"I am not a bitch: I am a good leader with high
expectations for myself and others."

What do you think about yourself? What is getting in your way? What do you think others are thinking? What are you afraid others are thinking? Does it matter?

As you can tell from this chapter and the survey, the words that we associate with ourselves are not always accurate representations of who we are. At some point, I realized that the positive words used in parallel with the "negative" words are actually how people I respect and care about see me.

For example, I would like to discuss my youngest daughter, Mikala. From the get-go, she has been fierce, and she's held her own in everything she's done. External sources (including her family) led her to believe that her weakness was her stubbornness. I know she says that about herself. When I look at her, I think she is stubborn because she is committed, loyal, and has strong convictions. It is not a weakness; it is a strength.

"Mikala is not stubborn; she is passionate and committed."

What I've taken away from the behind-the-mask journey is that I should believe in myself the way those I respect and care about believe in me. Nobody can be as mean to me as I am to myself. The words that we tell ourselves can only hold us back when we don't embrace the truth behind them.

Let's rewrite or reframe your self-beliefs.

- Ask yourself, *Which of these self-talk words or phrases do I tell myself?*
- Write them down.
- Journal on a situation where you or someone else might label you with one of these behaviors, and it actually means you are doing something right.
- Then change the word from negative self-talk to what you actually are.
- This is something you can do even as a reflective way to get through a tough business situation.

How do I take the negative self-talk and translate it into what it means to me and those I care about? Well, years of reflection and writing this book have told me:

I am a good leader.

I am strong, stronger than I know.

I am loyal to a fault. :)

I am trustworthy.

I am confident (even if I have to *earn* it until I *learn* it).

I'm good at lifting others up, and it feels great.

I am passionate, and it's okay to get emotional.

So many leadership books, seminars, and self-help guides talk about how not to care what others think of you. But this is much easier said than done. I've concluded that I don't care what everyone thinks—I care what the people I respect and care about think.

Give this a try!

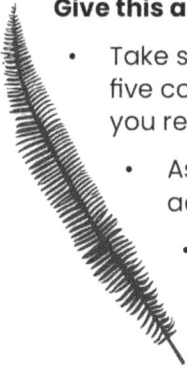

- Take some time out of your day to reach out to three to five colleagues, business associates, and friends that you respect and that you know care about you.

  - Ask them to give you three to five one-word adjectives that they believe describe you.

    - Take these words and add them to a word cloud.

      - If you feel inspired by it, you can frame it. I have mine in my office.

CHAPTER 9
BEING A WOMAN AND A LEADER IS COMPLICATED

I went to the *Barbie* movie begrudgingly. My daughters wanted to go, so I wore my pink and went. (Did you know that popcorn with butter is free of calories when you go to the movies!) I will acknowledge that the movie triggered some politics, but one monologue stopped me in my tracks. I thought, *Wow, that is it. That is the entire problem. The expectations placed on women are contradictory and complicated.*

"It is literally impossible to be a woman. You are so beautiful, and so smart, and it kills me that you don't think you're good enough. Like, we have to always be extraordinary, but somehow, we're always doing it wrong.

"You have to be thin, but not too thin. And you can never say you want to be thin. You have to say you want to be healthy, but also, you have to be thin. You have to have money, but you can't ask for money because that's crass. You have to be a boss, but you can't be mean. You have to lead, but you can't squash other people's ideas.

You're supposed to love being a mother, but don't talk about your kids all the damn time. You have to be a career woman, but also always be looking out for other people.

"You have to answer for men's bad behavior, which is insane, but if you point that out, you're accused of complaining. You're supposed to stay pretty for men, but not so pretty that you tempt them too much or that you threaten other women because you're supposed to be a part of the sisterhood.

"But always stand out and always be grateful. But never forget that the system is rigged. So, find a way to acknowledge that, but also always be grateful.

"You have to never get old, never be rude, never show off, never be selfish, never fall down, never fail, never show fear, never get out of line. It's too hard! It's too contradictory, and nobody gives you a medal or says thank you! And it turns out, in fact, that not only are you doing everything wrong, but also everything is your fault.

"I'm just so tired of watching myself and every single other woman tie herself into knots so that people will like us. And if all of that is also true for a doll just representing women, then I don't even know."
– America Ferrera's Barbie Speech

Three ideas are always circling in my head: **earn** it while you **learn** it, **FIO,** and **impostor syndrome**. In a way, each feeds the next. Where does one begin, and the next one stop? It feels like they are constantly circling in my mind.

*You can't **earn it while you learn it** if you do not just **FIO**, and that immediately makes you feel like an **impostor**.*

*While you are **FIO**, you will feel like an **impostor** if you are **earning it while you learn it**.*

*You can feel like an **impostor** from just thinking about **earning it while you learn it** and **FIO**.*

You get my point. It's complicated and all tied together.

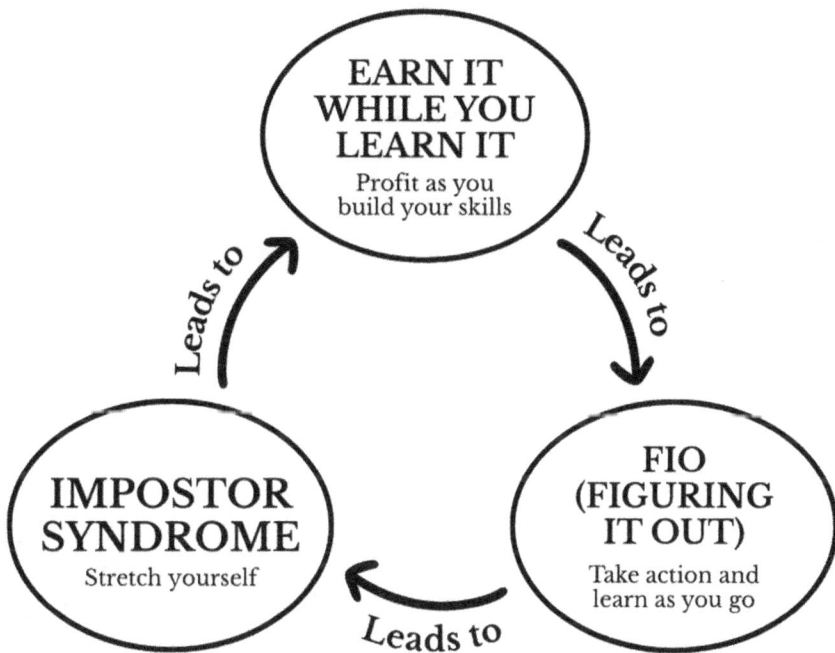

```
            ┌─────────────────┐
            │   EARN IT        │
            │   WHILE YOU      │
            │   LEARN IT       │
            │  Profit as you   │
            │  build your skills│
            └─────────────────┘
    Leads to ↑              ↘ Leads to

┌──────────────┐              ┌──────────────┐
│  IMPOSTOR    │              │    FIO        │
│  SYNDROME    │              │ (FIGURING     │
│ Stretch      │  ← Leads to  │   IT OUT)     │
│ yourself     │              │ Take action and│
└──────────────┘              │ learn as you go│
                              └──────────────┘
```

In the small but targeted survey I conducted, over sixty percent of respondents reported that they felt impostor syndrome was what was holding them back. For me personally, when you have a background of learning from life, it is almost impossible not to feel like an impostor. But let's be clear: we all have our own backgrounds that pull us into this mind-fuck. If you are interested in growing all the time, you will constantly put yourself into positions you are not quite ready for, so impostor syndrome is also a saying we need to reframe. I remember being in meetings and thinking things like:

What is he talking about? I need to write that down and learn all I can about that subject.

Hopefully, nobody will notice I am not supposed to be here. Just look confident and engaged. Maybe they will not notice I am out of my league.

Who would want to read a book about my experiences? I have not done anything special.

Did he just roll his eyes at me? Did I say something stupid? Did anyone else notice?

I remember being at my first big executive offsite and walking outdoors during a break. The sun was sinking, and there was a nip in the air (I remember this because I could see my breath). I stood there, taking deep breaths, looking at Mt. Bachelor in the distance, and thinking, *I am so thankful to be here, but what if someone notices I shouldn't be?* I had a tear in the corner of my eye.

Out came the facilitator, who said, "Good morning. I wanted to share with you that I have been working with this group for a long time, and your feedback and contributions are very valuable. I can see a difference in how the entire group is working together."

So, there I was, having a pity party about how I hoped nobody would realize I was figuring this all out and **earning it until I learned it**, and the only person who thought I was an impostor was me. As she walked away, I thought, *Michelle, cut yourself some slack. You are bringing value to this group without even knowing it!*

At one point in my career, I worked for a company that strongly encouraged its employees to get involved with the community. I was encouraged to get involved in areas where I was passionate, and the company would support me in many ways, including providing time off from work and donating to the organizations I was passionate about. It was a unique opportunity that I look back on with pride and appreciation.

One of those opportunities was serving on the Commission on Children and Families. This position was appointed by a circuit judge and required a significant amount of time and energy. The organization received funds from the state, donors, and through fundraising efforts. They used those funds to invest in other non-profits supporting the community. My background in marketing enabled me to think creatively about how to reach the community and increase donations and exposure for the organization.

Much of the work we did focused on two areas. The first was "fishing upstream," so to speak. That meant investing resources in early intervention, before children developed more significant problems. The other focus was on educating the community on how to either seek help or offer assistance. It was called: *Get Help or Help Out.* In that volunteer role, I worked on a multimedia campaign that included TV commercials, radio spots, newspaper ads, billboards, and more. We even won regional awards for the campaign.

While I was donating my time to this cause and others (on company time and with their support), a trend emerged nationwide regarding how companies could support their employees in philanthropic efforts within their communities. The work we had accomplished in the community caught the attention of the University of Wisconsin. They invited me to present to a group of their community leaders on the successes we had seen in Bend, Oregon.

Let me paint the picture for you. This was a paid speaking engagement. I had led many projects but had never spoken in public, let alone been paid to do it! The presentation room was located in a sophisticated lecture hall equipped with the technical ability to switch between Power-Point, audio (for radio commercials), and TV. Presenting a multimedia presentation and discussing the subject matter was very intimidating. Remember, they paid for me to fly, stay, meet with community leaders, and give a worthy presentation.

As they introduced me, I sat at the front of the dark audience with my legs shaking, on the verge of a panic attack. The thoughts running through my head were, *What the f@#$ were you thinking? You have no right to be here speaking to these successful business leaders. You are just a marketing person in a small town, with no real training or degree to back up what you are presenting. They will know you are out of your league. You are an impostor!*

I unsteadily walked up the stairs and tried to hold back my heavy breathing. I said, "Good morning. My name is Michelle Marquis. I am a working mom who leads marketing at a small but impressive real estate company. They have encouraged me to push myself and make a difference everywhere I can. This is part of that journey. I have never had the opportunity to speak to a group like this, so bear with me and think about who in your organization could be me. Think about what effect you will have on them and your community if you encourage philanthropy activity in your employees."

I started to calm down (I think by setting the expectations low for the group) and sailed through my presentation smoothly and with passion. The organization surveyed the attendees, asking, *"Will you do something different in your community because of what you learned here?"* Ninety-nine percent of the attendees said they would. **I earned it while I learned it**. My impostor syndrome had been overcome for that moment, but it is never far away.

I know many women who have the same sort of negative self-talk: *I do not know enough. I am not smart enough. I am not enough to do*

_____ .

I was conducting a training not too long ago where one of the women said, "I feel like I'm an impostor. It's very difficult for me to speak up." I was surprised. I knew her background and had to remind her of the reasons why she had every right to speak up.

I said, "Wait a minute. Didn't you..." and gave her a list of reasons she should feel confident in speaking up, even if she is stretching (FIO factor), until she could be completely confident. To me, it is like stretching a muscle. Every time you stretch, you get more limber. If you wait until you're ready for these roles, it's going to be too late.

I have put myself in so many positions where I have thought, *Pay close attention and learn this so they do not realize that you are an impostor.* I have worked hard to teach myself to identify my gaps as I see them. Sometimes, this meant immersing myself in self-training through reading books, conducting internet research, and seeking out mentors. I have an extensive library of great books that I now consider the foundations of leadership. I love them all so much that I added a chapter dedicated to resources for my fellow leaders to read within this book.

To have impostor syndrome is to feel that you do not deserve or did not earn a position, and are afraid to say the wrong thing. Sometimes, you are in a position because you 100 percent earned it. Other times, like me, you have either had to be an impostor until you could FIO or doubted yourself even when you "earned" the role.

I have come to believe that there is a bit of healthiness in being an impostor if you do not let it stop you! For me, it meant that I was stretching to do things I wanted to do or that I was forced to learn something new. Men take risks in life, whereas women often wait until they are "ready" for the opportunity. If we are constantly stretching, we will always find ourselves in uncomfortable positions. I am starting to embrace that feeling. It means I am learning and growing.

Being a woman leader comes with numerous hurdles. I have heard strong, extraordinary women leaders who are at the top of their game say that they are not taken as seriously as their male counterparts. I know at least two women who dyed their hair from blonde to brunette, hoping to be taken more seriously as they grew in their careers.

There were so many times that I thought to myself in a meeting, *Just be involved with solving problems and being part of as many solutions as possible, and they will not suspect that you do not belong in the room.* I'm not talking about early on; I'm talking about two weeks ago. Those thoughts have been with me all of my life and are still "renting space for free," as Andrew McConnell says in his book *Get Out of My Head.*

We are works in progress. Stretch. Embrace.

Men generally don't get impostor syndrome. They apply for jobs for which they're not qualified and take on the roles before they're ready. They do not have the same internal voices telling them they are not enough. Women tend to wait to apply or go for a promotion they "think" they are not ready for. As I think back on life, when I did/do have some self-doubt, it didn't stop me from jumping at every opportunity, even if I was not ready. I wanted to grow (and be respected) in whatever I did, so I constantly set myself up for challenges, like I was stretching a muscle.

Sometimes, I took roles that were not offered to me; in other words, I filled the gap until I was recognized as someone who could handle complicated areas without being told what to do. I was sometimes criticized as going too fast...and that I needed to slow down to let others catch up. I **might** still get this feedback. But as an employer once told me...I would rather have a thoroughbred that I have to rein in from time to time than an ass that I have to kick in the butt.

I have always looked at my willingness to jump in and solve business challenges I knew little about as "faking it until I made it." Some have said that faking it until you make it is not being authentic or even seems a little disingenuous. However, the more I thought about it, the more I realized that I am not faking it; I am learning the position, title, or role as I earn it. So, I am officially turning the mantra on its head, from "fake it until you make it" to:

You are not an impostor—**"You are earning it until you learn it."**

To learn it, you will have to jump in with both feet and FIO. Don't complain that you are not getting the roles you deserve. Evaluate what you do not know for a role, project, or promotion you want, and start to learn it. This will give you the confidence to show that you know more than you even know or are letting on. We discussed how men often take on roles they are not qualified for or ready for, but women tend to come up with a list of reasons they are not qualified to pursue them. Stop now. **Let's earn it while we learn it!** Apply for a title (and compensation) that is higher than where you are now. Many women I know are performing the duties of the upgraded role, but without the accompanying increase in income or title.

Maybe we need to change how we look at what being an "impostor" means. The self-talk is something we have 100 percent control over, but remembering you are earning it while you learn it will allow you to cut yourself some slack. If you are stretching yourself, you will always be the underdog in meetings, projects, or new positions. There are also ways to learn as you go. If you want to get good at something, you can always FIO.

At one time in my career, I found myself responsible for marketing at a resort in Bend, Oregon. At that time, successful marketing campaigns were conducted through newspaper ads, direct mail to potential customers, trade shows, and even television and radio commercials. The internet quickly came to life for finding lodging around 1996, with search engine marketing (SEM) and search engine optimization (SEO) hot on its heels. (What does that jargon mean? It means having online exposure for your website.)

I taught myself how to make sure the businesses I was running were found before those of my competitors when our customers were using the internet to find us. It was so interesting to me. Websites were new to the travel industry. The ecosystem for search was complicated. There were as many as eight or more search engines, with Yahoo leading the way. Today, there is one major player: Google. I knew that if I could master how to build a good website and ensure we were found before our competitors, I could help drive traffic to our website and almost own the digital space in my market.

At that time, very few web marketing companies actually understood how to implement the strategies being discussed in the circles I was learning from. Things were moving quickly in that industry, and unless you dedicated time to understanding it, you would be left behind. Most web companies were building websites, but not working on attracting more visitors.

I sent myself to what I ended up calling "SEO school." It really wasn't a school, but I treated it like one. I read everything I could find and attended a couple of SEM conferences, hosted by the renowned Danny Sullivan (IYKYK). I basically taught myself the best practices for SEO and SEM. This meant that I was able to take the company I was working with forward more quickly than any of my competitors, because even those who claimed to be SEO experts or website design experts were unaware of many of the things I was doing. I recall meeting with a website company that held weekly meetings with me to learn what I had picked up on my own.

So, embrace the impostor and do not let it stop you. Just FIO and **earn it until you learn it**. I made myself more valuable to the company and my career. Make sure you are constantly growing and challenging yourself. In most jobs I've ever had, I've been referred to as a Swiss Army knife because I would just fill in the gaps where needed. I've been winging it and earning it as I've gone along my entire life.

Apply for the job that you think you're not qualified for, take the project, lead the group, learn the new way, or foster a cross-functional group. Be the go-to person. Do not let impostor syndrome stop you from stretching and just figuring it out. If you are not taking roles, projects, speaking engagements, or even writing a book before you are 100 percent ready and then feeling like an impostor, do it anyway! **Earn it while you learn it.**

At a very young age, anything I didn't know, I had to fake it until I made it or pretend to know about it. I literally had to go into everything I did with confidence, be as quick a learner as possible, and not let them see me sweat. I had to keep educating myself because I was frequently in a role I was not quite ready for.

I had no formal training in leadership, sales, marketing, or budgeting. This meant I had to create or take on the roles I wanted early in life and in my career. I took on more roles than you could imagine by simply doing some of the job and proving I could do the role. I had to speak with authority even if I wasn't *the* authority on the topic. Being bold and speaking up is uncomfortable for most people, let alone a young lady.

When I share with people that I did not graduate from college, they are usually surprised. There is an assumption that to achieve high levels of success or to have positions similar to what I have "taken," I must have graduated with some sort of college degree. I was enrolled at one time, but my focus was not on school; instead, I prioritized having fun and ensuring I could be on the beach during tanning hours, rather than starting classes too early after a fun night. I never gave a thought to: *What will I be when I grow up?*

By the time college came around, I had already supported myself while in high school. Now I had to find a job that supported college, something I was "supposed" to do. I enrolled in classes on topics I thought were interesting, but with no aim to finish in a certain amount of time or with a specific focus. I was a kid, and **figuring this out** was harder than the other option: having fun. So, I was more focused on being in the moment.

That did not mean I was not ambitious. In every role I had, from renting jet skis on the beach to slinging cocktails in a nightclub, I was focused on the end result. I realized that the more I sold, the more money I would make. At one point, I was working at a crazy nightclub. The manager put together a promotion that tracked the number of pre-dinner cocktails (in dollar volume) we sold, as well as the number of desserts. At first, it was a competition I wanted to win. What it led to was me earning more tips than I had ever earned before. As the price of each ticket went up, so did my commission (tips).

Through this merry-go-round of **earn it while you learn it**, FIO, and being an impostor, I traveled the world twice, bought my first home, and led a team of forty before I was twenty-five years old. Oh, and by the way, when I traveled, both employers saved my job for me, saying, "Just come back." One of them did not even move a picture on my desk. That is how much some of my employers valued the job I did for them.

While I was living in Hawaii, the company I was working for decided it wanted to grow their revenue further and started a destination management company (DMC). DMCs work with corporate travel planners or incentive companies who bring groups to Hawaii. The DMC is responsible for planning all the details of events, including transportation, activities, tours, functions, and logistics.

First of all, I had never worked at a DMC and only understood a small piece of what they did, but I raised my hand and I said, "I'll do it!" As usual, when an opportunity to grow presented itself, I did not hesitate to take on the challenge, despite having no prior experience or understanding of what it really meant to "do" the role. I would do it as I had done most things in my life: I would just FIO!

Take a minute to think of all the pieces that needed to be put in place to build out that business. I had no collateral, no procedures, and no contacts to fulfill the services. I didn't know how to charge, bill, or hire for the events. So, I was agile before it was "hip" to be agile. This means I literally developed these things as I went. Nothing was perfect, but with constant improvement, we achieved great success.

But first things first: I had to get customers. By the way, there was no internet back then, so I purchased a book with lists of meeting planners and incentive houses, and then started "dialing for dollars," one name at a time. I went to work each morning, picked up the phone, and called each person on that list until I hit the right one, learning as I went who that person was and what I needed to say to get them to not just take my call but listen to my pitch.

One of those names was the purchasing manager with Carlson Wagonlit Travel (now, CWT). They were located in Minneapolis, Minnesota. I cold-called him (remember, again, there was no internet, so no research; this was truly a cold call). I have no idea what I said or what prompted him to take my call, but I did tell him I would be in the area meeting with other incentive houses and would like to include him in my meetings.

Setting the picture again: I was twenty-five years old, with long blonde hair, wearing my Hawaiian dress and little black "slippahs." And it was March, which meant there was not only snow on the ground but freezing temperatures. I didn't even own a coat. I think I had a sarong (a very thin piece of material in a Hawaiian print) around my shoulder to keep me warm.

As I pulled up in the taxi cab on what is the Carlson Wagonlit Travel campus, I saw a large sign displaying all the companies they owned, including Radisson Hotels, Carnival Cruise Line, and TGI Fridays. They were the largest travel company in the world at the time. My stomach fell to the floor. *Michelle Marquis, what did you get yourself into?* I had no understanding of just how large this company was. I had chicken skin (goosebumps) all over my arms.

I walked up to their large corporate headquarters, obtained my security badge, and waited for the director of purchasing to come and get me. Then I was led into a meeting room with a group of people (all men) sitting around a board table. Intimidating, yes. Doubting myself, yes. I had printed copies of a "brochure" with what I thought would resonate with someone bringing groups to Hawaii. I then just spoke from my heart about the business we were building. I shared the vision of where we were going, but never mentioned that we were actually just starting the business.

The whole experience was life-changing because, on a professional level, this was the furthest I had pushed myself to do something so foreign. Did I get the business? Yes! We ended up being their preferred supplier on the island of Maui for all the events they planned there. Could you imagine if I hadn't just gone and figured that out and pretended that I knew what I was doing? We would never have gotten that business.

How did I have the courage? *Because I did not know I couldn't be successful.* My mom had never shown that she was not capable of doing whatever she set her mind to. As you can imagine, my relationship with my mom has been complicated, but no matter how upset I get at some of her decisions, she was also one of the original kick-ass, bossy leaders. She and I have had long talks about how she was able to accomplish all she did with so many things stacked up against her.

My mom shared with me that she was raised to be a wife and mother. Her upbringing focused on how to entertain, have manners, and set a table (she went to college to find a husband, not an education). She went on to say that when she became a single mother at age twenty-eight, she had no idea what it meant to support her family. She did what most women did during that time: she became a secretary. She faced many biases—working mom, divorced, no job in years—but in the end, she

figured it out. At that point in my life, I had just done what I'd had to do, so why was this any different? It wasn't.

Every time you FIO or **earn it until you learn it**, you will have a chance to make a mistake, which quickly catapults you to feeling like an impostor. But the risk is worth it.

I was working with a resort in Bend, Oregon, that had one small meeting room and one event room. I had come there from a resort in Sunriver with lots of meeting space, where I was doing group sales. They wanted me to develop a group sales program using just those two small rooms. Again, I had no experience actually building out a program, let alone servicing the groups I sold to. It never occurred to me that I had never done anything like this. I just started.

I quickly demonstrated how, with that small meeting space, we could generate a substantial amount of bookings and revenue for the company. So, I started pitching the idea of building a conference center on some vacant property we had. I brought it up at every opportunity. At one point, I remember the general manager saying, "Damn it, Michelle, we'll probably never build this thing. Stop pushing." But I kept the pressure on.

Finally, they asked me to prepare a pro forma for the conference center. A pro forma? What is that? I had never created a business plan that also included a five-year pro forma. I had to FIO. What's it going to cost to build? What's it going to cost to purchase chairs, AV equipment, and glassware? What does the kitchen need? What will it cost to run it? How much revenue will we bring in? How long will it take to make a return on our investment? What would a five-year forecast look like in billed revenue, net profit, and gross sales? I literally drew my idea for the meeting space on a napkin in front of the architect. I just **figured it out**.

Once I had prepared the pro forma, I was then asked to present it to the board for approval. Again, I found myself in a meeting room with the entire board sitting around the table when I arrived. All but the general manager were men. Was I nervous? Yes. Was I intimidated? Yes. Did we get the investment to build the conference center? Yes.

Now, about two weeks after this was approved, I was going over the expense numbers, and I noticed that I hadn't loaded the labor costs. What that means is that I had not included any employee taxes, insurance, 401(k), etc., in my modeling. Labor costs included sales, marketing, catering, banquets, the convention center manager, and other expenses. It was a lot of money that I had not loaded with any benefits. This added another 17 percent to the costs, which would mean our ROI would be off by quite a bit. My stomach just dropped. I was sick. It was after hours, and I called the CEO of the company I worked for, holding back tears, and told him of my mistake.

He said, "That's okay. We all make mistakes."

I was blown away. It was the first time I understood what a great leader was.

My point is that you have to push yourself to do things you have never done, or you will not grow. Being an impostor can be a good thing! My impostor syndrome shows up at the worst times.

For example, I was at a conference in the short-term rental industry. It was one of the first times I had spoken in front of this group, and there was added pressure because it was also the first time my new boss would hear me speak. I was well prepared—I had practiced, and I had all my notes on cards, perfectly aligned with the slideshow. I knew what I was talking about and had a plan to follow the notes with each slide. I wanted my new employer to know he had hired the right person.

The night before my session, I fell ill. I took NyQuil and slept hard. I woke up still feeling sick, but now I was also drowsy. I felt terrible, but the show had to go on! As I walked onto the stage, I dropped all of my note cards. When I picked up the note cards, I started to breathe heavily and got dizzy. I literally had a panic attack on the stage in front of my peers, clients, and my boss. I don't know how many people knew I was going through this, but it felt like I might faint. Ten minutes passed (well, it felt like ten minutes, but it was probably only ten seconds) as I collected myself. I said to the group, "Just a minute." Then I turned my back to the audience, took a sip of water, and took a few deep breaths.

When I turned back around, I saw a gentleman sitting in the front row. He was a tall man with a handlebar mustache and big ol' boots. He looked at me and said, "You got this girl. You know your stuff. Just speak from your heart." I took a deep breath and did just that. I put my slides down on the table, looked at them, and spoke to what I believed was the point of each one, no note cards. I knocked it out of the park. That gentleman was Sandy Stone, and he eventually became a mentor and, in time, a good friend.

This is where nurture overcomes nature. Nurture says, "You just have to stretch, FIO, and earn it while you learn it!

As you know, because this story is where I decided to write this book, I had the opportunity to speak to a group of women in the industry I work in. I had never done a keynote speech. At this point in life, I'd done lots and lots of speaking, but to speak to a group of four hundred women about flipping all of these adjectives in their heads made me feel very, very raw and vulnerable. I had never spoken in this style before: no slides, no interaction with the audience, just talking for thirty-five minutes. So, I started by telling everybody that I was impostor-*ing* and pretending to be a successful keynote speaker. By the small laughs and whispers, I knew the crowd understood. This opening gave me a bit of courage and reminded myself that being an impostor was a good thing. I was growing.

"I'm not an impostor. I'm a constant learner, and I'm pushing myself to grow every day, including today. I will not let 'not being ready and not knowing everything' stop me from stretching to take on new challenges."

CHAPTER 10
AGILE LEADERSHIP

T his chapter is titled "Agile Leadership" because I believe your leadership style will change drastically over time and with experience, and that is a good thing. You are putting yourself out there, making mistakes, learning from them, meeting people, learning from them, reading and gathering experience, all while learning from those things. You will learn to put things in place, act differently, and then make gradual changes and improvements over time.

What does it mean to be an *agile leader* versus just a *leader*? A quick internet search defines "agile" in terms of software development.

In software development, "agile" means a flexible, iterative approach to project management and software delivery that emphasizes collaboration, continuous feedback, and adaptability to change. It's not a single methodology, but rather a set of principles and practices that prioritize delivering working software in smaller, manageable increments.

Let's rephrase this for leadership:

In leadership development, "agile" means having a flexible, interactive approach to relationships and leadership that emphasizes collaboration, continuous feedback, and adaptability to change. It is not a single methodology, but rather a set of principles and practices that prioritize leading a team by building strong relationships in small increments.

It was not until I had led a product team that I understood not just my life as a leader but also how much I had grown through years filled with growth lessons, all of which tied back to being agile. I was an agile leader. I took things I learned, applied those lessons, and made small iterative changes.

It was not done purposefully, but as I experienced life. I am no longer building my career, but I remain a constant learner in areas that I believe will help me become a better person, mentor, and leader.

Take a moment. What are you doing differently today because of something you learned yesterday? Are you being intentional? I was not, and boy, I wish I had paid more attention to this. If I had, there would have been a lot less collateral damage over the years.

Someone once told me, "Michelle, you leave a wake behind you." When I heard it for the first time, I did not get it. But after hearing it again, I did what I do with anything: I dug into how I could not leave a wake but have people join me on the wave.

The first step is admitting you have a problem, right? So many women leaders feel like the only way to lead is to "take charge" and be that proverbial "bull in a china shop."

I have had many conversations where women leaders say things like:

- "I am a bull in a china shop, and the people I work with just need to understand that."
- "I say what I am thinking. People need to understand that I am just being truthful and that the truth hurts sometimes."

Sharing this type of information with people you work with is just a protection mechanism and, if I am being honest, an excuse to behave poorly. How you make people feel is a big part of being an effective leader.

I have been called a bulldozer, a lone wolf, and even a bull in a china shop. I might have gotten things done quickly, but I did it without a team supporting me. They say that hindsight is 20/20, and it really is. Over time and with experience, I have come to recognize a few things about myself, and when I do, I go to work on them, just as I do with everything. I FIO—I did all I could to be a better leader. Incremental improvements.

There is a widely recognized saying:

"If you want to go fast, go alone;
if you want to go far, go together."

Honestly, good leadership can be learned. It's not always something you're born with. There are certain traits and characteristics that form the foundation of a strong leader, and those can be developed over time.

I've found that personality tests can give some insight into whether someone has natural leadership tendencies. Not everyone's personality fits the typical leader mold, but certain profiles seem more likely to lead the way.

Most leaders I've known tend to lean toward the "hard-charging" side—like being High-D or High-I on the DiSC chart, or seeing themselves as Mavericks or Captains, based on the Predictive Index. The thing is, many of these leaders, especially those with High-D traits, don't always have high emotional intelligence naturally. So, a lot of us have to put in extra effort to develop those softer skills—stuff like empathy, listening, and emotional awareness.

That's definitely been true for me. It's a journey of growth, not some innate trait you're born with.

I was hard-charging from early on. As I look back, I believe this is because I had to take the lead on decisions and projects so I could learn what I did not know before others could see that I was an impostor. Consequently, a few things slowed me down in my pursuit of being a great leader.

For one thing, I always had the hardest time giving kudos to someone doing their job. I think this is because I have always had to just get shit done, with nobody telling me what to do or cheering me on. There were no gold stars for doing what I had to do. Nobody ever told me, "Good job, Michelle! You paid your rent." "Good job, Michelle! You went to school." "Good job, Michelle! You scored a goal in soccer." "Good job! You paid your insurance." Or, "Good job! You got a job."

So, it felt disingenuous to me to give kudos to people who did what they were supposed to do—their job. I thought, "You get paid to do your job, so why do you need kudos for doing it?" Again, that was just how my experience had impacted me.

I have dedicated a significant portion of my career to developing my leadership and confidence skills. Aside from mentorship and reading books, I've also gotten certified in the five appreciation languages of work.

I had to find a way to be candid and truthful, while also encouraging people to be open to hearing me, because I had enough in my relationship bank to withdraw from. As a way to be intentional in showing people I appreciated the things they contributed, I started the practice of wearing bracelets on my left arm and moving them one at a time over to my right arm when I deposited into somebody's emotional bank. This helped me be intentional and conscientious about making this a habit and part of my leadership approach. If, at the end of the day, I had bracelets on my right arm, I knew I had led with purpose. I did this until it became a habit. I still wear my stack of bracelets, but now they are a reminder to me of my growth.

My ongoing learning also extended to developing leadership skills. As I mentioned earlier, one of the companies I worked at conducted 360 reviews and skip-level interviews. All the feedback I received clearly indicated that there were a few areas in which I could improve.

One of these was using emotional intelligence to lead people according to what motivated and inspired them. I had read a book called *The Five Love Languages*, which was about relationships with significant others. It made such an impact on me that when the authors released a book on appreciation languages in the workplace, I delved in. When I read it, the list did not include physical touch, but it has been added since then.

- Words of Affirmation
- Quality Time
- Acts of Service
- Tangible Gifts
- Physical Touch

The general idea of the book is that every person has a preferred way of receiving appreciation. Normally, without specific effort, people express appreciation in the same way that they receive it, which leads to people not always feeling appreciated. People will follow you to the ends of the earth if they sincerely feel that you appreciate them and deposit the appreciation into their emotional bank.

The book rang so true to me that I got certified in the philosophy—and boy, did it tell me that I was doing some things wrong.

For example, I worked with a salesperson who was fantastic at what she did and how she did it. She was a sponge when it came to learning and would take on any project with enthusiasm. She was a pleasure to lead. I wanted to make sure she knew just how highly I thought of her, so I went to my go-to. I felt appreciation through words of affirmation (remember, this piece was and still is something I work on with others) and tangible gifts. This meant that I was not only trying to constantly let her know that she was good at her job and call her out publicly, but I would also do little things, such as giving her a gift with a special note. I always tried to make these gifts meaningful.

However, after I read *The Five Appreciation Languages in the Workplace* and did my certification, I realized that her appreciation language was quality time. So, there I was, giving her gifts, writing her notes, and building her up, while what would motivate her would be for me to take some one-on-one time with her, listen to her ideas, and ensure that I was including her in decisions and such. I was doing the wrong things to inspire her.

Part of being a good leader is also about staying inspired. About seven years ago, I was going through a difficult time, both professionally and personally. In an effort to get centered, I went to a yoga class with one of my biggest supporters and bestie: Christi. Time with her always makes me feel better. You have to have those relationships in life!

I was at my favorite part of yoga, savasana—you know, the mini-naptime. Instead of napping, I lay there with tears running down my face. As I was leaving, I overheard some women talking about a book by an author named Brené Brown, called *Daring Greatly*. They mentioned a few points from her book that resonated with me. I thought, *Hmm, I need to take a look at that,* and I put that name on the back burner. That is what my mom called it when you wanted to think about something, but not right at that moment.

Later, I was on social media and saw a friend share her top reads for the fall. At the very top of that pile was *Daring Greatly.* I thought, *Huh. Okay, note to self again. That's two.* Then I had two additional women (both in leadership in my community) share that they were doing Brené Brown workshops. Okay, too many coincidences to ignore. I took those items from the back burner and moved them to the front. I started with her TED talk and was hooked. If you haven't seen it, I highly recommend doing so as soon as possible.

I took a three-day workshop based on her teachings and learned a great deal about what was holding me back from being not just a good leader, but a great one. Some of the things I have shared in this book were clearly holding me back. One of Brené's lessons is about being the one who dares greatly, which is from a speech given by President Theodore Roosevelt. I have this speech on a board in my office to remind me what it is like to be the one doing the hard work every day:

"It is not the critic who counts; not the man who points out how the strong man stumbles, or where the doer of deeds could have done them better. The credit belongs to the man who is actually in the arena, whose face is marred by dust and sweat and blood, who strives valiantly, who errs, who comes short again and again, because there is no effort without error and shortcoming, but who does actually strive to do the deeds, who knows great enthusiasms, the great devotions, who spends himself in a worthy cause, who at the best knows in the end the triumph of high achievement, and who, at the worst, if he fails, at least fails while daring greatly, so

that his place shall never be with those cold and timid souls who neither know victory nor defeat."
– Theodore Roosevelt, "Citizenship in a Republic," Sorbonne in Paris, France, April 23, 1910

This was a great lesson for me and an example of learning as I go, being agile in response to the results of my actions, and re-engineering how I lead.

CHAPTER 11
MENTORSHIP AND GROWTH

have written about how earning it until you learn it and FIO are some of the foundational ways to grow into a strong leader, but the advice would be incomplete without also sharing how mentorship can help you accelerate your skills and life lessons. Mentors have "been there and done that" in different areas of their lives than you, and their life experiences are different than yours. In my life, they have guided me through numerous important and pivotal times, from how to structure a compensation plan for myself to talking me off the proverbial bridge when I felt like I had nowhere to turn and no one to advise me.

Not all mentors know that they are mentors. As parents, our kids watch everything we do. This is no different when you are in a leadership role. When you work or have relationships with young people (anyone younger than you are now), they, too, are watching what you do, not usually what you say. Do the right thing. Lead by example. Do what you know is right. Young, aspiring people are watching.

Being raised by a single mom who was the original #bossyleader and #badass meant I had seen firsthand that you could do anything you set your mind to. From a young girl's point of view, the things my mom modeled were just part of our lives. I knew nothing different. As an adult, I realize that raising the two of us, attending law school, and working three jobs to pull it all together must have been very hard for her. She never made it look hard, but it must have been a challenge.

She was not raised by a working mom; in fact, her mom, my grandmother, was a socialite. She was the mom from *Leave It to Beaver*: perfect house, perfect family, raising perfect children. My mom's memories of her childhood were those of living a simple and sweet life. Things changed for her when her father, Grandpa Austin, had a mental breakdown. It was then that my grandmother had her own experience with FIO. She was always fashion-forward, so she opened a clothing boutique in Pacific Palisades in 1965. My memories of my grandmother were a combination of strict manners and rules, as well as her running her business at the clothing store. She was a complex woman, and I have so many great memories of helping where I could: organizing shoe sizes, making bows, and hanging clothes. For me, she was a mentor and role model.

Both of these women were mentors to me, without them even knowing it. I would not be the woman I am without them. My girls do not realize it, but neither would they. My mother and grandmother paved the path for future generations of our family by boldly resisting the societal pressures of what it meant to be a woman (in leadership roles).

So, who shaped your hustle? Think back to the people in your life who gave you that extra oomph without even knowing it. For me, there were also teachers, other people's parents, and friends of my family. Open your journal and write down who those people were and are. Then think about who you could be a mentor to.

Over the last five to ten years or so, there has been considerable discussion about the benefits of having a mentor or coach. I have had the opportunity to work with both coaches and mentors throughout various stages of my life and career. So, what is the difference between a coach and a mentor?

A coach is someone you work with on specific skills or tactics that are measurable. For example, I work with several companies to audit, evaluate, and then coach their team on specific tactics, where the results of that work can be measured through data. This work usually takes two to three months.

A professional mentor is generally not attached to the results of your relationship, so their views are more neutral than speaking to a friend, co-worker, or even a family member. They provide an outside point of view, and not only can they be someone you can vent to, but someone who will ask you the difficult questions about how you plan to change your situation. These relationships can last for years or maybe even a lifetime.

I have had sales coaches, life coaches, relationship mentors, and just people I knew I could trust with some of life's most important quandaries. I would not have had such success in my life without these relationships. Some of the mentors I have had over the years were not "official" ones. We never discussed it, and they were never compensated; the relationships simply evolved over time. Some of those amazing relationships have turned into mutual mentorships. I trusted them to give me the hard truth and tell me where I needed to grow. We all have gaps, some of them more like caverns, that need to be filled.

So, you have a choice:

To do it all on your own and learn from your mistakes, possibly over and over again.

Or

To work with someone who has been where you want to go.

I call this a shortcut, a way to learn from people who have walked that path and can help you see hurdles or things that might get in your way.

When selecting a mentor, it's important to find someone who complements those gaps but is also someone you can relate to. I have heard women say that they feel awkward getting a mentor. My question to them is this: if you were going somewhere and you got a little lost, wouldn't you ask for directions, even from a stranger? Most reading this book would say that they would. Asking someone might be a little awkward at first, but once you do, you will get where you are going faster! And you get to decide what your relationship looks like with your mentor.

How can you find and ask someone to mentor you?
Start with journaling on the outcome of what you are looking for in a mentor: a promotion, a raise, a new job or role, life balance, deeper skills, or maybe all of that. Who do you know that you respect in your life, industry, or community? Make a list of those people and then compare them to your desired outcome. Which of them could fill the gap and fill your cup?

It is not too often that a mentor charges for their time, so when someone agrees to be your mentor, they are usually doing it out of the kindness of their heart and because they believe they can help you grow both personally and professionally. They will decide the time and mental space to focus on you. It is your responsibility to do the hard work and be prepared for each meeting. You are asking somebody who is probably very busy to take time out of their day to be your mentor, so be ready to be engaged.

My first mentor worked with me in all areas of my life. Cotty taught me how to change people's first impression of me from a twenty-four-

year-old surfer girl to a leader or executive. She made a significant difference in my growth as a leader. She started by discussing how to dress for
meetings (I wish I'd worked with her before I went to Minneapolis for
my first meeting with Carlson Wagonlit Travel). The company I worked
for and that sponsored my mentor even paid for a shopping spree, and
she took me shopping for "looks" to make me not only feel the part but
look it. She worked with me on communication skills, not sweating the
small things, and how to identify the root cause of issues. I have been
fortunate to have a few very good employers. They invested in me in so
many ways, but in part, as mentors, too.

However, I want to acknowledge this: be careful with both
employers and peers at work. Not all employers are truly interested in
you as a person, but rather in how you can serve them. So, when you
share too much, they can use that information against you. Hindsight
tells me that I got too close and was too honest with a few of my
employers or colleagues, which ultimately hurt our business relationship.

So, how do you know whom to share things with? Before trusting
them because you like them and they seem to like you:

- Watch their actions, not their words.
- Ask yourself, *Do they share confidential information about others?*
- Also ask, *Do they take responsibility for their own mistakes?*
- Make sure that they don't "guilt-trip" or pressure you to act
  on things you have already told them no about.
- Ask yourself if you ever have to second-guess their behavior
  or actions: *What does he/she mean when they say that?*
- Identify any times they might have made you "feel special"
  but then treated you differently in front of others.

> **Who do you trust in your professional relationships?** Is there anyone with whom you question your alignment? Pay attention to your intuition. It is probably right. I wish I had done that more.

I have had two coaches in the last ten years who have had a positive effect on me, both personally and professionally. One was a gentleman named Luke. He excelled in sales leadership, but he was even better at evaluating situations and approaching things from a fresh perspective. He also had a knack for communication and was great at helping me navigate difficult conversations and situations. He helped me troubleshoot some of the very tumultuous professional situations I had, and even assisted me in navigating a very emotional departure that truly changed the trajectory of my professional career.

Another coach, Amber Hurdle, has helped me through PR nightmares, writing speeches and supporting me in a way I never experienced before meeting her. When I speak to her, I think, *Yes, I am in the right spot, doing the right things.* She will probably kill me for sharing this, but she has done this as a friend, not a paying coach—I think because we enjoy each other so much!

How do you find one? Usually, your peer network can help you find someone in your industry or who focuses on women, that sort of thing, so that you align with them quickly.

If you hire a coach or mentor, you should expect a structured conversation on how you approach things, setting goals, and similar topics.

CHAPTER 12
THE BIGGEST LIFE LESSONS

As I look back, I wish I had paid attention to all of the lessons life was teaching me along the way. When I struggled, I felt so alone. I had clues that the unconscious negative self-talk of not being enough (enough to love, enough to be worthy) was completely false. Each story, experience, and interaction gave me pieces of a puzzle that took way too long to put together. The reality of who I am and what I have overcome, shared, and learned is bold. I am stronger than I ever knew (something my mom has always said I am).

When I think about all of my life's lessons, I know I would not be the person I am now without them. If I could pick out any one lesson that affected me the most, it was probably when my mom asked me to move out when I was seventeen. It was the original thread of my entire blanket of experiences that led me to where I am today. Was it easy? No? Many hard things are forged through necessity, and not all are bad.

I recently came across a list of eight pieces of life advice I wish I had known at a younger age. I agree with all of them and added some flavor to each.

1. **Even when you trust someone,** keep some things to yourself. You do not have to share everything.
2. **If you want to build something worthwhile**, be ready for criticism. Not all criticism is bad.
3. **Your mental health** is far more important than your career will ever be.
4. You become an unstoppable force **when you realize you can do it alone. But also realize that you do not have to do it alone!**
5. **Be okay with people not liking you.** Most of them don't even like themselves. That makes it very hard for them to like or love others!
6. Not everything will go according to plan, so **be ready to adapt**. And that is okay. Agility in life means you will never be perfect.
7. **You can always choose to be happy**, no matter what happens in life. Being sad should never be an option. This is *far* easier said than done, especially if you have any poor mental health genes.
8. Don't waste your time stressing about the **things you can't control**. It only robs you of today and changes nothing for tomorrow.

What are the truths that life has taught you the hard way, but that you're better for learning? I asked some of my Support Squad what their biggest life lessons were as strong women leaders. Here is the advice they gave:

Judgment & Perspective: Good thoughts, good words, good deeds. Take control of what you say to yourself. You just might believe it.

- "Don't assume ill intent."
- "Don't judge a book by its cover."
- "Do they really know you? Then why care what they think?"

Self-Worth & Courage: Have the courage to be the author of your own story.

- "Don't worry about what others think."
- "Don't be afraid to be bossy or loud or to speak your mind."
- "Being true, open, and honest matters more than being liked."

Emotional Resilience & Optimism: Anxiety is often a reaction to living too far in the future. Come back to now, where your feet are, where your breath is, where your power lives (Buddhist saying).

- "You don't have to be sad. You get to decide how to think about it."
- "Hard things shape you—they're not always bad."
- "The glass is always half full...of wine."

Opportunities to remind yourself of how you want to live your life come around all the time. Intuition and serendipity are not coincidences. You just have to pay attention.

One day, my husband and I were in line getting gas. Both lines had cars in them. In one, vehicles were fueling up, but in the other, a big van was sitting in the middle of the lane, blocking both pumps. We grew frustrated with the person who had parked their car that way and discussed how inconsiderate they were. The longer we waited, the more indignant we became at how rude that person must be.

All of a sudden, from behind us came a guy in a wheelchair. He wheeled himself to the front door of the van and waved. Then he pulled himself in and leaned out the door to disassemble the wheelchair, bringing each piece into the van one at a time. The silence between my husband and me was deafening until I started to cry. We were both ashamed and drove home in silence.

On our way home, we were on a dark, winding road. Someone coming at us flashed their lights three or four times, blinding us. We both thought, *What jerks.* As we came around the corner, there was a herd of deer on the road. The people in the other car had been warning us. We went home in awe of the life lessons we had learned that day. The memory of these events comes back to me just about any time I start to judge a situation or a person.

I attended a conference years ago, and the keynote speaker was someone I had not heard of before. I read the description, saw the picture, and immediately judged the speaker. *What a waste of time,* I thought. *What could this young woman in the tall leather boots teach me? She's a good thirty years younger than me. What could possibly have happened in her short life for her to teach me?*

Big gulp! She was not only very experienced in life, but in ways I was not. She brought so much to each and every person in that room. She was wise beyond her years and not because of her life experiences but in spite of them. Michelle, do not judge a book by its cover. Do not judge others. Do not compare yourself with others. The life lessons just keep coming.

When I think back to both my grandmother's and my mother's strengths, those lessons also stand out, but in a good way. Yes, they made difficult decisions and decisions that are part of the fabric of my life. They were not "lessons" per se. They were just life for me. My mom worked hard, went to law school, and raised two daughters—all on her own. Why wouldn't/couldn't I be a #bossyleader with great success? For most of the time, I did not know the odds were not in my favor.

Another important example for me was just how fiercely independent both of my maternal role models were. Independent does not mean "by oneself." To me it means to be strong and not afraid to lead and GSD (get shit done). As I raise my daughters and granddaughters, I hope each of them feels that strength from me. It will allow them to be confident and independent and to find their own way to be a #bossyleader.

It is funny, though; my daughters continue to teach me life lessons as well. When my mom says to me, "How did you get to be so smart? I am so proud of you," I now get it because I feel the same way about my daughters. As I raised my daughters, I tried to teach them what I believe are the core values that are most important to Brian and me:

- Integrity: It is the key to an authentic life (IYKYK).
- Reliability: Do what you say you are going to do.
- Loyalty: Know who you are. Family first.
- Fairness: Treat people like you want them to treat you. Treat everyone the same.

When I see my girls in action, I know that these traits are an integral part of their character. My first granddaughter, Hunter, is showing signs of being fierce, fearless, and independent, too, and I could not be more proud.

Journaling Challenge: What are your biggest life lessons? How have you applied those lessons in life? Who imparted those lessons to you? If you were going to give life lessons to a younger version of yourself, what would you say? Write your younger self that note.

Dear Younger Michelle,

There is so much I want to share with you, but probably the single most important point:
Don't worry so much. It does not help!
Don't worry if everyone likes you. They don't, and that is okay!
Don't worry about what others say or think about you. The ones that know you won't talk about you, and the ones that don't know you and talk about you - who cares?
Don't worry about money. Just keep doing what you are doing. The money comes.
Don't worry about whether you are doing a good job. You are. You know you are.
Don't worry if you are enough. You are. Trust me.

Believe it.
Love, MommaM

When I think about life lessons, it sounds like you get the lesson, and then you move on. Life lessons evolve with you. Back in Chapter 10, "Agile Leadership," we talked about how you learn as you go and make things better as you have more information in front of you. Life lessons are the same way. As recently as a few months ago, I had an old lesson come back and say hello to me!

I woke up and meditated. The sun was shining (I live in Washington state, so this is not as often as I like), and it looked like it would be a great day.

Then I had a prospective client who had committed to a project that went cold (I wasn't good enough to secure the business). A company I was working with was two months in arrears on what they owed me, and they were not calling me back (I was going to end up being homeless; I know, a bit dramatic). Also, someone I thought was a friend (and peer) completely cut off communication with me (They didn't like me), and my daughter shared some things that she was worried about (every mother worries about their kids—though they say, "Happy wife, happy life," the truth is, "Happy kids, happy wife").

I went from feeling like I had a great day in front of me to being worried, stressed, and almost obsessing about the what-ifs with each situation.

I had a boss who once told me, "Michelle, you know it always works out. Just be patient." And Buddha said, "Worrying does not take away tomorrow's troubles. It takes away today's peace." So, I let my brain go quiet. I took a deep breath and re-evaluated each thing that had come to me.

With the prospect who had gone cold:

- What I used to think—*They do not think I can do the job.*
- What I changed my thoughts to—*If the client does not hire me, I will just find another client.*

With the company that was two months in arrears:

- What I used to think—*Will that money make it so I cannot afford [X]?*
- What I changed my thoughts to—*If the client never pays me, lesson learned, and better to find out now than continue to work for them.*

With the friend (and peer) who cut off contact:

- What I used to think—*They are mad at me. I did something wrong.*
- What I changed my thoughts to—*My "friend" is not a true friend, and I have to stop investing in that relationship.*

With my worry for my daughter:

- What I used to think—*How can I fix it so she is not worried?*
- What I changed my thoughts to—*She is going to be fine. She just needs me to listen and support her.*

CHAPTER 13
DO I HAVE TO CHOOSE TO BE A MOM OR GO TO WORK, OR CAN I DO BOTH?

C an we nurture our families while also nurturing ourselves and our careers? Can we have it all? First of all, all moms are working moms. Let's blow up that bomb right away. There are many types of working mothers, and each is no more important than the other; however, I will focus on the mothers who work outside the home. I do this because this book is targeted at women who are leading now and those who want to lead in the future.

Let's be honest with ourselves: you will miss out on things if you choose to work. You will also miss out on things if you choose to stay home. The choice is difficult, but in many situations, it's not really a choice at all. For me, it was a little of both. My skills had me in a position to make a great living for my family, and at some point, I started out-earning my husband. This created a dynamic that was difficult to navigate. At times, I felt resentful for not having a choice in being the bread-winner. Now, after saying that, I also knew I liked to work. I derived a significant portion of my self-worth from working. I think both my husband and I were resentful about the situation, each for our own reasons. This was a lot to navigate, and it took hard work on both our parts for us to find our way in our roles.

Then there was the guilt of not being a "normal" mom. That's so funny to think about now because I was not raised by a normal mom, so what made me think I should fill that role?

I do not know of a mom who has not felt guilty at one time or another for missing something in their children's lives. For the first ten years of my youngest daughter's life, my husband and I both worked. That meant I also cooked, cleaned, grocery shopped, paid the bills, and saved time to play with the kids. In all reality, I was working two jobs. My youngest, now twenty-seven, does not remember any of that. All she remembers is that I was a working mom and not home much. She remembers the things I missed, not the things I did to be everywhere all at once. I know she is proud of the woman and leader I have become, but the guilt of not being where she had hoped I would be is something I still struggle with.

Probably the *one* good thing about COVID was the flexibility it gave the entire country to work from home and deliver results rather than punch a time clock. I was beyond raising my kids at that point, but it was clear that having children around was no longer taboo. This makes it easier to have a blended life.

The data on working mothers supports the fact that many have chosen to have a family while advancing their careers. The Pew Research Center found that in 1969 (when I was a kid), only 11 percent of women were the breadwinners in their households. Today, that number is close to 50 percent. The percentage of working mothers in the United States is close to 73 percent (Bureau of Labor Statistics).

I have been fortunate because I had employers who allowed me to work from home all the way back in 1992. I had just had my first daughter, and they wanted me to have a work-life combination that would allow me to be with my daughter as much as possible and still be a high contributor. They were way ahead of their time. I remember dragging the desktop computer and monitors (no laptops back then) to and from work.

At one point, I had an employer who let me leave work early three days a week to coach my daughter's soccer team. He just knew I would get my work done, regardless of where or when I did it.

For many years, the world has discussed the importance of having a balanced life. I do not believe that is possible. I had someone share with me the concept of a blended life. This made so much more sense because a balanced life says you're going to give equal time to everything, and you can't possibly do that. You just can't. However, a blended life suggests that you'll change hats at different times of the day or on different days.

That means that you go and coach soccer on weekday afternoons, and if your child is sick, you stay home. However, it also means that if you have an important project that needs to get done on Saturday, you do it on Saturday. So, work and life aren't balanced so much as they're blended. I've always lived that, and I've had employers who have been very supportive. They focused on the outcome, not the time or location I was at.

Below is an example of what blending work and life might look like. In the diagram, you can see three different examples of how you can dedicate plenty of time to get work done, but also set aside space for your personal life on any given day.

Blended Work-Life		
Can Look Like This	Or This	Or This
Life		
7:00–9:00		Work
Work	Work	7:00–11:00
9:00–12:00	7:00–3:00	
Life		Life
12:00–1:00		11:00–3:00
Work		Work
1:00–6:00	Life	3:00–5:00
Life	3:00–10:00	Life
6:00–10:00		5:00–10:00

I know I worked more than my fair share of hours, but I also know I was lucky enough to have employers who supported me while I nurtured my children and my career as much as possible.

What could I do to have a more blended life?
Is my employer open to this?
How do I speak to them about this?

CHAPTER 14
RESOURCES FOR GROWTH

I n this book, I discuss mentorship, forming a squad, and learning from life lessons. I have also leaned heavily on reading self-help books. Sometimes, I just need to get out of my head. I look back at my previous journals and recognize patterns. Those patterns need to be broken. The growth needs to happen within me as well as around me.

For me, there were three different types of growth books I gravitated toward. I started reading books (and articles, and now listening to podcasts) as a way to fill the gaps in my knowledge. That journey began in earnest when I became an individual contributor. I read nearly every well-regarded sales book I could get my hands on.

I then began changing my behavior based on what I read. Not every book "spoke" to me, but many included pieces that aligned with behaviors I already had, so what I learned was easier to adopt. And lo and behold, my natural sales ability became supercharged. That's when my employers started placing me in sales leadership roles. The thinking was simple: if someone is good at sales, they must also be good at leading salespeople. That's not always true, but in my case, it was.

The challenge came with the second part of sales leadership. It required leadership, and that was an area where I needed to grow. Once again, I turned to books to help me learn how to become a better leader. Those leadership books eventually led me into the world of personal development.

To this day, there hasn't been a book or podcast I've read or listened to that didn't offer valuable ideas and insights I could implement to become a better person, leader, or team member. The life lessons I picked up were reinforced and, in some cases, softened by the lasting impressions these books had on me.

Take a look at some of my favorites in the personal development space, books that helped fuel my leadership growth.

Mindset Reset

This book helps you challenge your inner dialogue and reclaim your power.

- *The Four Agreements* by Don Miguel Ruiz
  - So simple. So effective.
    - Be impeccable with your words.
    - Don't take anything personally.
    - Always do your best.
    - Don't make assumptions.

Two ideas in this book hit me square in the eyes. The first is **don't take things personally**. I *wish* I had embraced this agreement as a mantra many, many years ago. Very little of my life was anything personal, but I took it as such. The other one that struck me was **don't make assumptions**. My story about the man in the wheelchair is a great example of not making assumptions. In the end, don't these two things cover everything we worry about in our heads?

> Which of these "agreements" do you break most often? What agreement do you want to recommit to starting today?

Emotional Strength and Vulnerability

This book reminds you that strength comes from owning your story, not hiding it.

- Anything by Brené Brown

Literally anything. Her research shows that vulnerability stems from a fear of disconnection. We think that if we show our weaknesses, people will see that we believe we are not enough. Her TED Talk, "The Power of Vulnerability," has been viewed sixty-seven million times!

In Brené Brown's book, *Daring Greatly*, she provided me with a framework to turn vulnerability, shame, and resilience into strengths. So much of my life was built on shame, not being enough, and caring too much about what people thought about me. (She calls those people the ones who take the cheap seats in your life.) Her book was one big ah-ha moment for me. So much of what I learned from her book and in her workshop gave me the confidence to leave a job I'd had for well over a decade and take the leap to start my own business.

Power, Presence, and Ownership

These books helped me step into my bold, capable, unapologetic self.

- *The Let Them Theory* by Mel Robbins

This is on all the charts of best reads, and when I read it, I thought, *Yeah, sure. Just let them. Sounds easy. Not! Like, just move on?* And then I heard a podcast where two psychologists discussed "The Let Them Theory" and how it aligns with setting boundaries in relationships. That is when I had my ah-ha moment for this book. The Let Them Theory is really about setting clear boundaries, primarily on what you let "get to you." If someone does not respect, value, or love you, they can use up your very limited and valued energy and further diminish your self-worth.

When a friend recently dismissed my feelings about something, I thought, *Let them. What they feel has nothing to do with me.*

- *Bombshell Leadership* by Amber Hurdle

The first time I heard Amber speak, I was skeptical as I waited for her to start. I had read her bio (very briefly), seen a picture of her, and made an *assumption.* What could this forty-something teach me? I have been there, done that. My life has taught me its lessons. Boy, was I wrong. So wrong. Her story was complete and funny, and she had done so much in her life. This told me that it is not the time you serve, it is the life you experience. We all have something to teach each other.

One of my favorite teachings from Amber is to name your inner critic. Amber's is "Gertrude." I asked AI for some help with naming my inner critic: Edna Not-Enough. "Edna" is a decrepit old lady wearing orthopedic shoes and shaking a finger at me. Her purse is filled with unreasonable expectations and unsolicited opinions. She is the self-proclaimed caretaker of the "You Are Too Much Club." She's too loud, too bossy, too ambitious, and yes, not enough, all at the same time. Now that Edna has a name and personality, I feel more empowered to just let them...

Accountability and Change

This book helps you shift from wishing to working—and from chaos to clarity.

- *Take Time for Your Life* by Cheryl Richardson

This book is not for the faint of heart. Be ready to hold yourself accountable for things that happen in your life, and if you do not make changes, do not expect anything to change. This includes cleaning out your closet and getting rid of things you collect that no longer serve you, including relationships.

When I read this book, I made peace with the things not serving me and literally "cleaned out" my life. I had friends who were taking more than they were giving, robbing me of my energy. This book challenged me. I took the challenge.

Other Resources

There are so many other business books I have read over the years that have made an impact on me. Those categories include professional development, organizational development, sales skills, and sales leadership skills. As you know, I did not attend college, so I have been earning it while I learn it, and reading is an important part of my education.

Another great educational opportunity is podcasts. The thing I love about them is that you can explore a specific subject and learn different perspectives from various individuals on it, or listen to a particular guest and delve deeply into a topic you're interested in, all at your own pace. Podcasts are almost master classes for me.

1. **Build Your Growth Stack:** Pick one of the books above. Read the first chapter and then write down three takeaways. Apply ONE of those takeaways in the next seven days.

   Then ask yourself:

   - *What changed?*
   - *How did it feel?*
   - *What did I learn about myself?*

2. **Build Your Own Resource Bank:** Create your own lifelong "Growth Toolkit."

   Ask yourself:

   - *What book changed how I see myself? If none, find one.*
   - *What podcast or voice makes me feel braver? If none, find one.*
   - *What mentor, friend, or coach do I turn to for truth?*
   - *What habits help me reconnect with my power?* Habits are not just a twenty-one-day effort but a lifetime of little incremental changes.

My growth and life lessons have come to me over many years. My only advice for you is not to wait so long to understand that you are enough. You are not an impostor; you are figuring it out until you can master it. You are *earning* it while you *learn* it. Use others' life lessons to enhance your own. Mentors, life lessons, books, and podcasts are all life hacks to help you move forward sooner—and with less regret.

CONCLUSION

A Zen Mantra

*"It is time to remind yourself of who you no longer want
   to be.*

Consider the choices you will no longer make,

behaviors you will disengage from,

experiences that you will avoid,

thoughts or emotions you will no longer embrace.

Release these aspects of your past with compassion,

understanding that they have served their purpose.

*Leave them in the past in order to fulfill the future version
   of yourself.*

*You are actively rewriting your mind and sculpting your
brain to align with your desired future,*

*to become defined by the version of your future self instead
   of your past.*

Feel your heart and mind aligning to the same frequency,

vibrating in harmony with one another.
This alignment is where you can tap into your true power.
You are not a passive spectator in your own life.
You are the architect, the creator.
The past does not hold the key to your future.
You have the innate power to create your reality,
to be whatever you desire.
Embrace the understanding that you are NOT limited.
You live a life of conscious and deliberate creation by step-
ping into your power.
You are shaping the world around you to mirror your
inner world.
You are limitless.
Consciously create your reality with power and intention."
– Jo Rose

Every single woman reading this book deserves to have it all. You're putting learning and heartfelt energy into expanding where you are today, so congratulations. Remember that you are not your experiences. You're a result of those experiences, and you can choose to be a victim or use them to build a house of confidence and resilience.

Flip the script on the memories of what made you who you are. You know, that little voice that says you're not good enough, the little voice that says you know who's going to read this, the little voice that says, "Why would someone want to hear anything I have to say?" With all those little voices, flip the script. Change those adjectives and cultural descriptions into powerful ones.

We are bossy—because we are good leaders who are not
afraid to...

We are emotional—because we are passionate and care
deeply.
We are abrasive—because we are candid and act with
kindness.
We are difficult—because we hold people accountable.
We are aggressive—because we push for resolution.
We are intimidating—because men do not know how to
"handle" us.
We are not impostors—we are constant learners and
pushing ourselves to grow every day.
We are not bitches. You're a strong, confident woman, and
people who do not understand that will always be
intimidated by you.

You should and could FIO as you grow. Don't take a role you already know how to do. Take a role that'll stretch you and then figure out the rest. Spend time with your Support Squad or mentors. Find your Squad, and they'll remind you who you are. If you're in doubt, ask them.

Writing this has been cathartic, and I am seeing that so much of my "bitchiness, abrasiveness, being emotional, aggressiveness, being difficult, and even being intimidating" was a coping mechanism. I went from having to be more than I was in the early stages of my life to using those skills to stretch and grow. That meant pretending to be confident, *knowing* my mind, and not letting anyone see that I was not in complete control of myself. I did not have any other option in my life (and it became *who* I was) except to just push through and FIO.

From very early on, and in every role I have ever held, I have had to earn it while learning it, and take every opportunity I wanted. I did not know there was a limit.

Build Your Credibility Pitch

This is not to share with anyone, this is to remind you just who the f@#$ you are!

I am Michelle Marquis.

My husband and I have used our life lessons to raise two strong women leaders. They are both wonderful human beings who are living their own happy lives.

I have had hard life experiences that have allowed me to share with other women the shortcuts and pitfalls they might encounter as they grow their leadership careers while still being moms and wives.

I have coached and cared for my various teams to the point that they have given me an endearing nickname: MommaM. I embrace that.

Take this challenge

Who are you? What do you stand for? Get all the negative thoughts out of your head and remind yourself about just what makes you a badass.

I appreciate that you've taken the time to read this book, and I hope just a small piece of my life lessons have shown you that no matter what stories are in your head (and we all have our own stories) and what culture or society thinks about who you are, flip them so that you see yourself in a positive light and not as the adjectives that society has said you are.

When I look back at that little girl waiting on the front step, I now realize I was always enough. My father not showing up had nothing to do with me and everything to do with his own shit. My life experiences were just small lessons that helped me understand just how strong and fierce I am.

You are not your worst day, but your best comeback. I have come back again and again throughout my whole life. You can, too! Start now.

THANK YOU FOR READING MY BOOK!

LET'S CONNECT!
Scan the QR Code:

I appreciate your interest in my book and value your feedback as it helps me improve future versions. I would appreciate it if you could leave your invaluable review on Amazon.com with your feedback.
Thank you!

www.ingramcontent.com/pod-product-compliance
Lightning Source LLC
Chambersburg PA
CBHW022010090426

42741CB00007B/971

*9 7 8 1 9 6 8 2 5 0 5 0 8 *